NEBRASKA

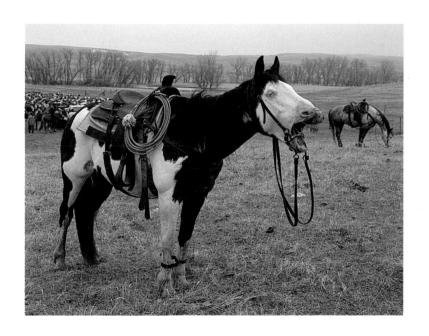

To John & Sharon

from
Tom & Jane
June
2011

CATTLE ROUND UP, WHITMAN

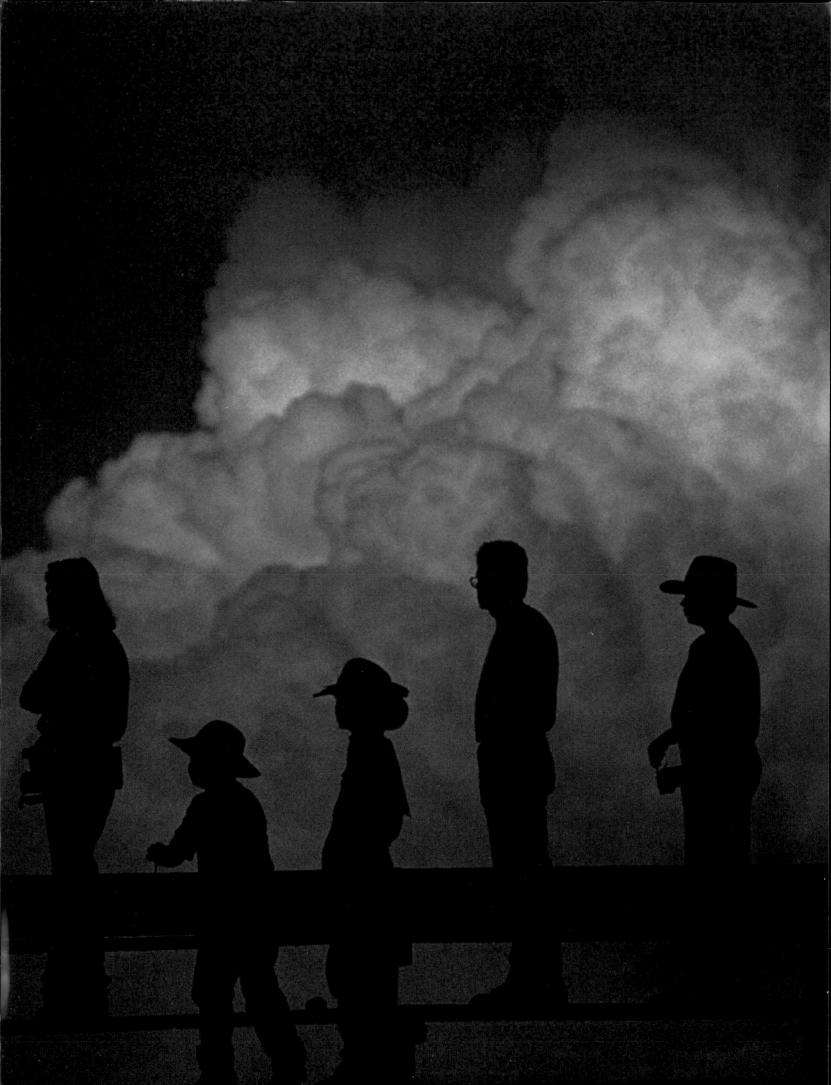

To my parents, John & Sharon Sartore,
for giving me a little common sense, a strong work ethic and a sense of humor to balance the two.

NEBRASKA
possibilities...endless ℠

Publication of this book was made possible with the generous support of the Nebraska Department of Economic Development's Travel and Tourism Division. For more information, log on to www.VisitNebraska.org or call 877-NEBRASKA.

preceding page
If there's one thing that photographers love, it's thunderstorms. In fact, you'll see several in this book. Big storms fill up our skies with color and excitement. This scene was shot at Nebraska's Big Rodeo at Burwell (that's the name the locals insist you call it, by the way).

First Nebraska paperback printing: 2006

Library of Congress Cataloging-in-Publication Data
Sartore, Joel.
Nebraska: under a big red sky / Joel Sartore.
p. cm. — (The Great plains photography series)
ISBN-13: 978-0-8032-5970-6 (pbk.: alk. paper)
ISBN-10: 0-8032-5970-0 (pbk.: alk. paper)
1. Photography, Artistic. 2. Photography—Nebraska. 3.
Nebraska—Pictorial works. 4. Sartore, Joel. I. Title. II. Series.
TR655.S28 2006
779'.99782—dc22
2006013712

under a big red sky

NEBRASKA

JOEL SARTORE

UNIVERSITY OF NEBRASKA PRESS

Lincoln & London

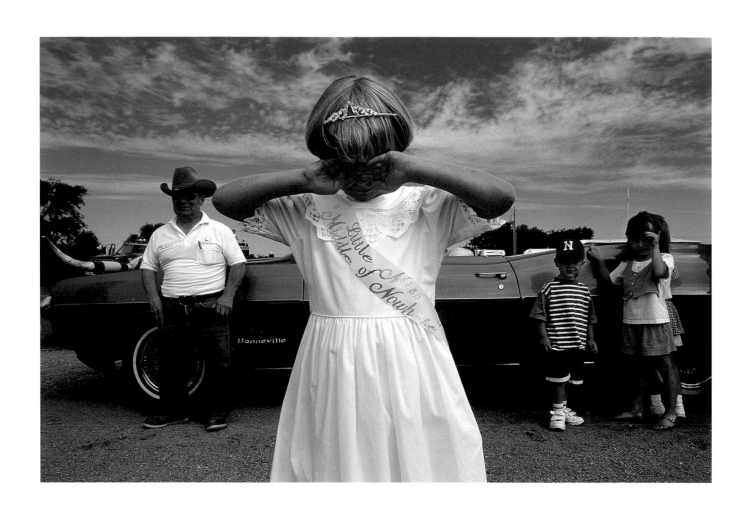

MIDDLE OF NOWHERE FESTIVAL, AINSWORTH

"I'm from Nebraska."

I repeat this phrase several times a week. Usually it's because I've met someone, somewhere, who's curious about the twang in my voice. Most folks just shake their heads in disbelief, especially if they're from the East Coast. "I flew over Nebraska once," they say. "It was brown and flat. I shut my window shade and slept." If they'll listen, I tell them about the people back home—how they smile and wave, needing no excuse to make conversation with a total stranger; how folks don't honk if you're late coming off a green light; how they take neighborhood walks at night without fear and think fast food is a treat.

I reaffirmed all of this for myself recently when working on a story for the National Geographic Society. The subject was my home, and from thunderstorms to prairie grass to the way we say "pop" instead of "soda," I learned a lot about the place I've lived all my life.

I grew up in Ralston, on the edge of Omaha but still rural enough to allow for a sense of independence. To me, it was Mayberry. The drug store had a soda fountain. The hardware store had a stuffed sailfish over the cash register and 20-year-old merchandise on the shelves. We also had a huge Fourth of July celebration complete with contests dealing in beauty, fire hoses, sky diver accuracy and alcoholic beverage consumption.

Our house was located under the final approach for Offutt Air Force Base. All through the Cold War, a steady stream of bombers, fighters and tanker planes rattled the lid of our barbeque grill as they slowed for landings. In all those years of grilling steaks, my dad never failed to look up.

In my town everyone knew each other's business. If someone got a new car, it was time to celebrate. If someone did well fishing, he displayed his catch out on his front lawn. We knew

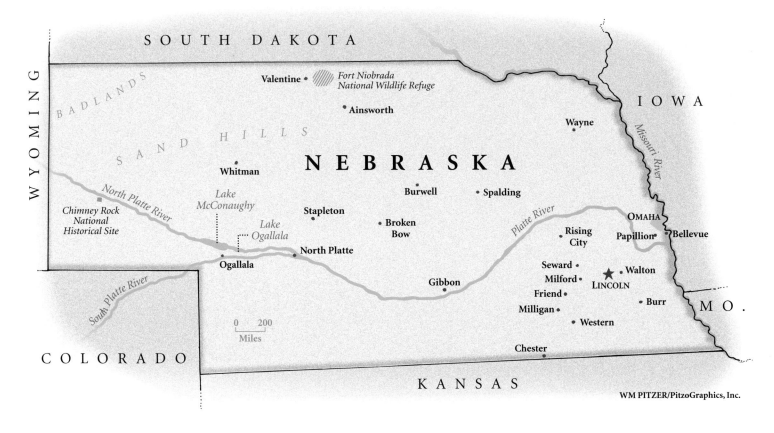

what our neighbors had for dinner, what their favorite TV shows were, what time they went to bed. There must have been comfort in knowing all this. We wanted it that way.

I grew up thinking Nebraskans were special people because we actually enjoyed living in a place with no big attractions like mountains or oceans. In fact, my family would never dream of going to a beach for a vacation. We went to the Badlands of South Dakota or some other hot, dry spot.

Our tolerance to the weather also makes us special. Very few places have the range of extreme heat and cold we do throughout the year, keeping those of lesser character from settling here. Spring and summer bring violent thunderstorms and tornado warnings, sending us scurrying underground. Winter means high winds and storms that routinely bury everything in snowdrifts. The roads gather potholes and salt. If you have a nice car, winter is not the time to drive it.

I learned cheap imitations don't count here. If a building is made poorly, the weather rips it to shreds. Deceitful people are treated the same way. They're not tolerated. Quality, honesty and endurance are what count. They anchor us.

Like many, I moved away right out of college. But after six years, I realized that this was the place that I wanted to live for a variety of reasons.

1. I've never heard anyone yell at anyone else in public here.

2. At the Lincoln airport I can tell at a glance if my flight is in. Odds are it'll be the only plane there.

3. Traditions count. Two of the nicest people I've ever met, my in-laws, go to the same lake every year even though the fishing stinks.

4. My group of friends dates back to grade school, and none have ever been divorced.

5. You can't beat the prices.

I went to an estate auction in Surprise. The last item up for bid was a two-story farm house in good shape that sat on a full city block. It was down to just me and one other bidder, a middle aged woman with a mean squint, and the bidding was fast and and furious in $100 increments. Then my wife leaned over and whispered, "Joel, if you get it, you'll have to mow it!" I let the place go at $7,000.

But now I've rambled enough. After all, this isn't supposed to be a "word book." It's just a picture book, not meant to be all-inclusive or even objective. It's simply one guy bouncing around in a beat-up Chevy truck, photographing the things that interest him. In the end, I hope the pages show only my admiration of the state that I call home.

Someone once said a photographer who gets good pictures out of the Great Plains can make good pictures anywhere, mainly because there isn't as much to shoot. Whoever said that didn't live in Nebraska.

The Nebraska assignment: a cheap date

For the first time in my life, I didn't want an assignment to be over. As a photographer for *National Geographic*, I usually couldn't wait for the tremendous relief that came with a shoot's end. Not this time though. Several years ago I'd proposed that we do a story on the state of Nebraska. Besides giving me a chance to explore my home territory, a story like this would allow me to spend a lot of time with my wife and two small children. And besides, the Society knew I'd be a cheap date for them if they allowed me to proceed. There was no plane ticket to buy, and I'd be sleeping either in my own bed in Lincoln or in the bed of my Chevy s-10. I was determined to be the least expensive photographer they had ever seen.

Now that the story has been published (*National Geographic*, November, 1998), I realize the personal rewards that came from it. This was a chance to explore and herald the state I'm always bragging about, a chance to finally have an excuse to shoot the giant covered wagon gas station near Milford.

All Geographic assignments work as a kind of carte blanche scavenger hunt. Time is the major constraint, its inaudible bell being the deadline. I had eight weeks to research and find the most interesting things I could within our 77,000 square miles. I could break up my assignment time over a one-year period in order to capture the seasons. Those were the only rules.

What would you cover if you were me? What's of critical importance, journalistically, to this state's economy, geography and culture? Personally, I'd rank farming, ranching and football, although some would want that order reversed. How about telemarketing? Five percent of Omaha is now calling you on any given evening. And don't forget that the nation's nuclear weapons are controlled through STRATCOM in Bellevue. Buffalo Bill invented rodeo in North Platte. Boys

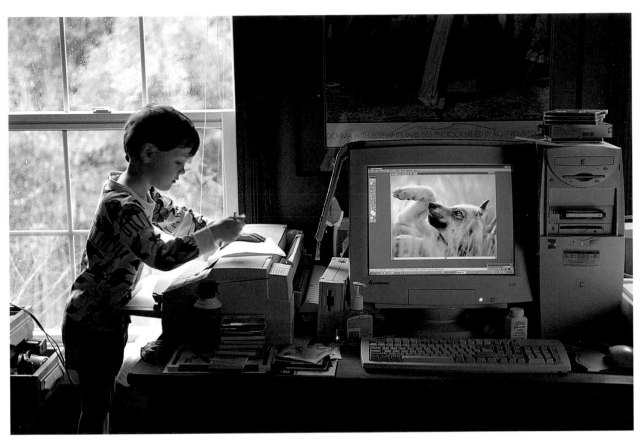

COLE WORKS ON HIS MEMOIRS IN MY OFFICE.

Town now takes girls and has gone global. Everyone's heard of Cabela's. There's only one Uni-cameral. Needless to say, I went way over my eight weeks.

There are not a whole lot of right or wrong answers when doing something like this, only a feeling that I hadn't done enough by the time I had to go on to my next assignment, a story on gray wolves (*National Geographic*, May, 1998).

I'm saddened that more of the faces I photographed in Nebraska didn't get published. These faces, down to the last man, woman and child, were caring enough to let me peek into their lives. They let me record their moments, but often we don't have the space to publish nearly enough. I hope they understand.

Today I've set out a few of those images for you. Sorted on my basement light table, they're just glowing spots of color, like our towns seen at dusk from the window of an airliner on its way somewhere else. But draw closer. See what I've seen— a wonderful place.

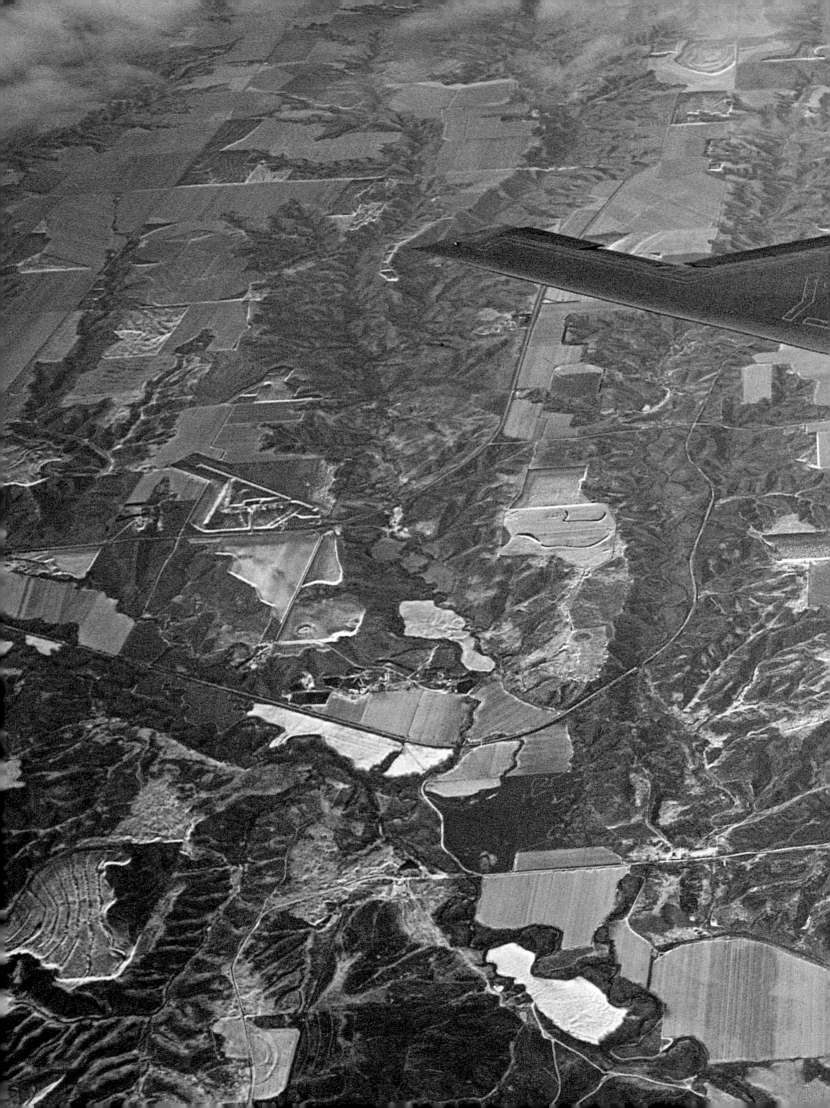

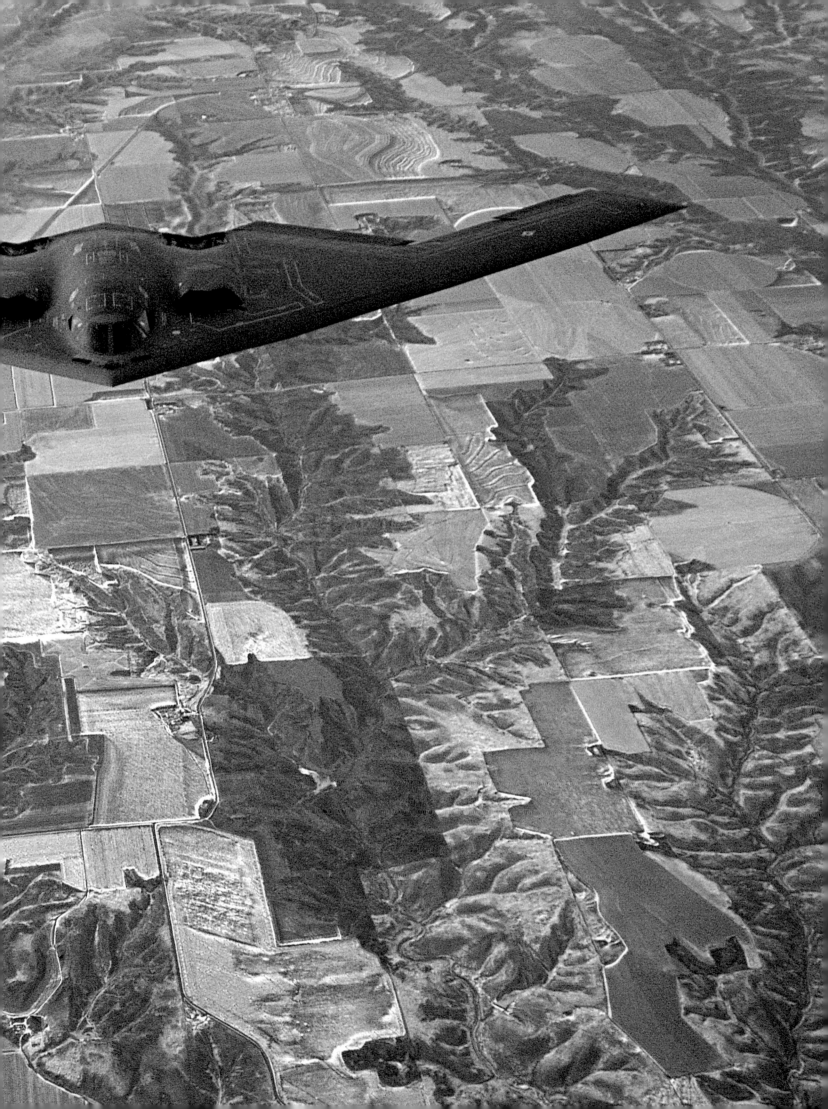

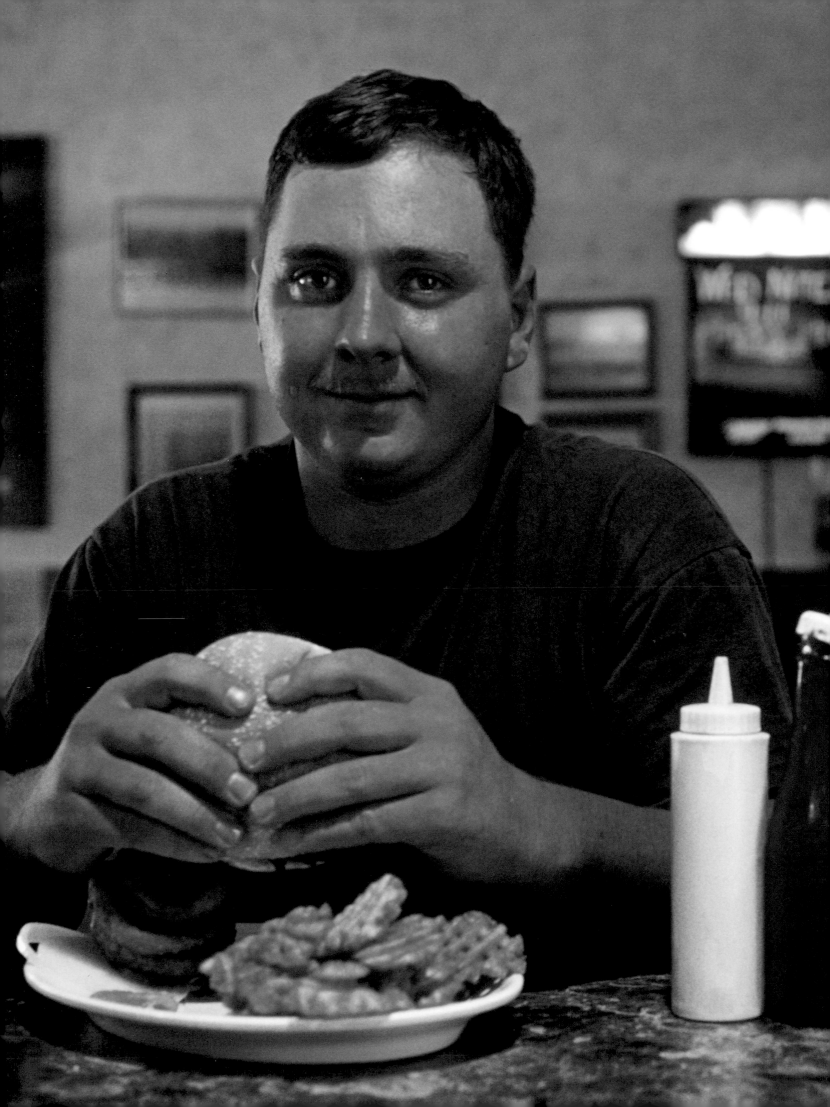

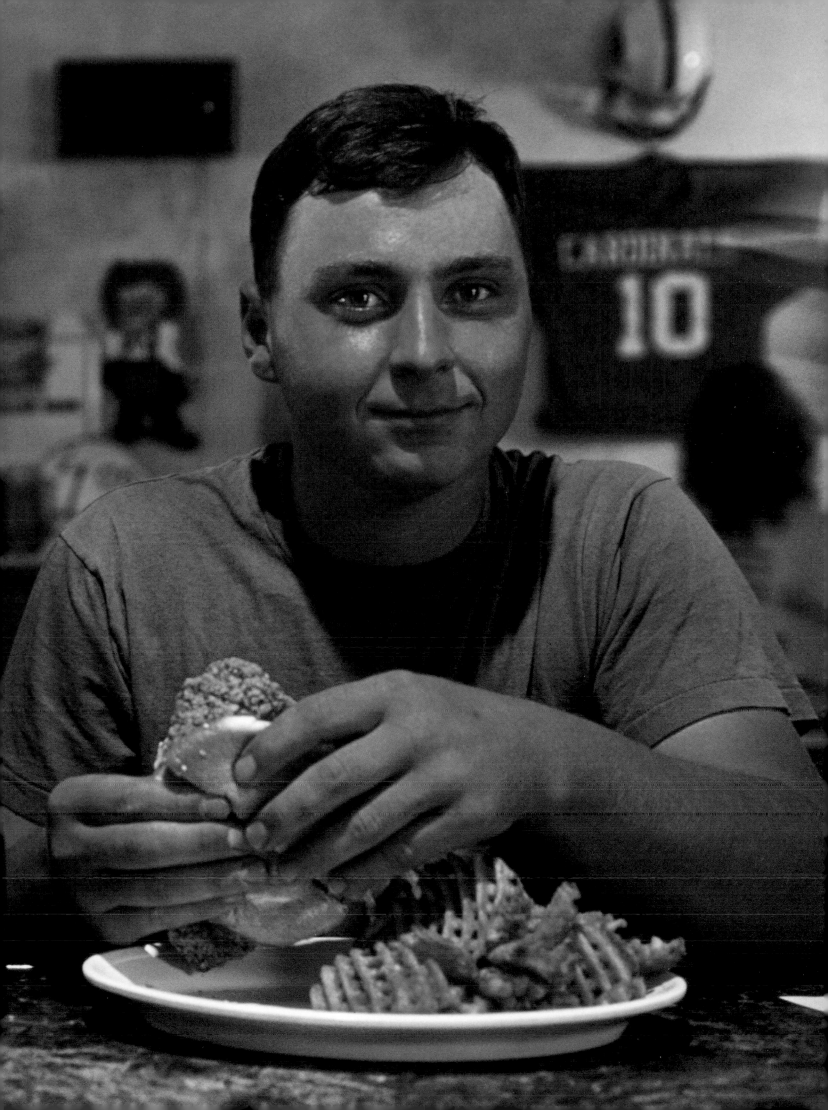

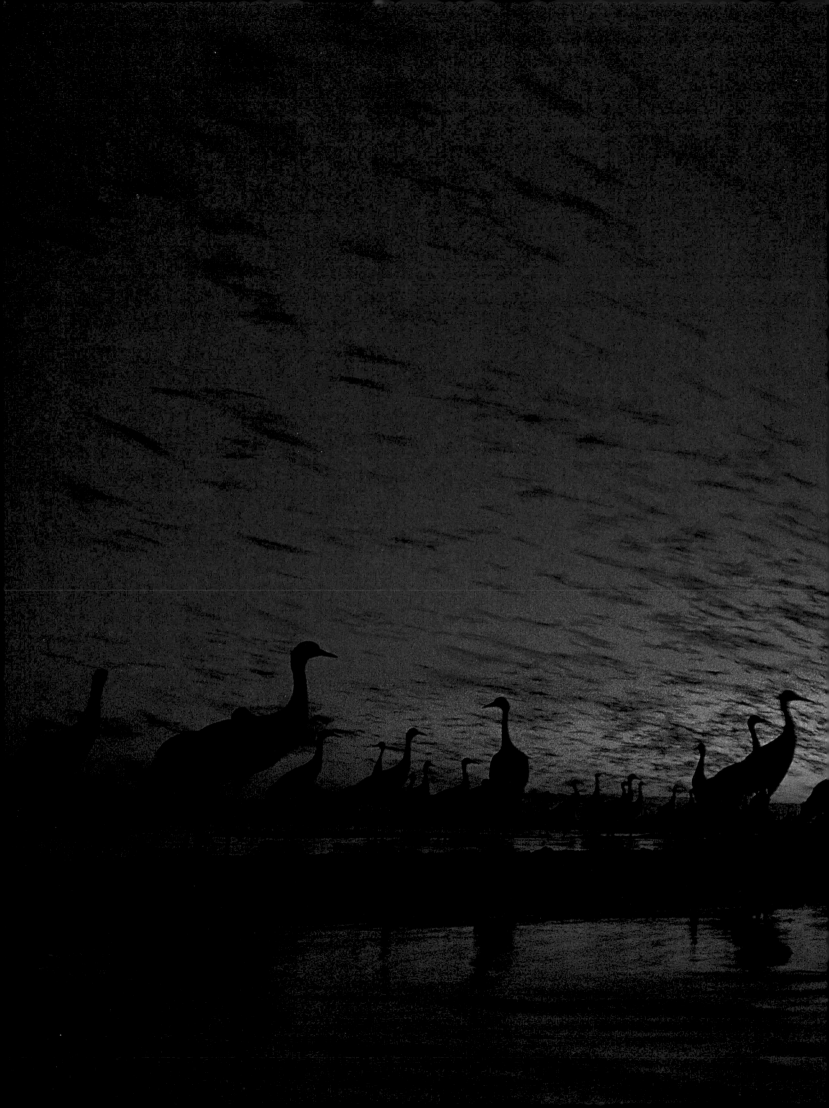

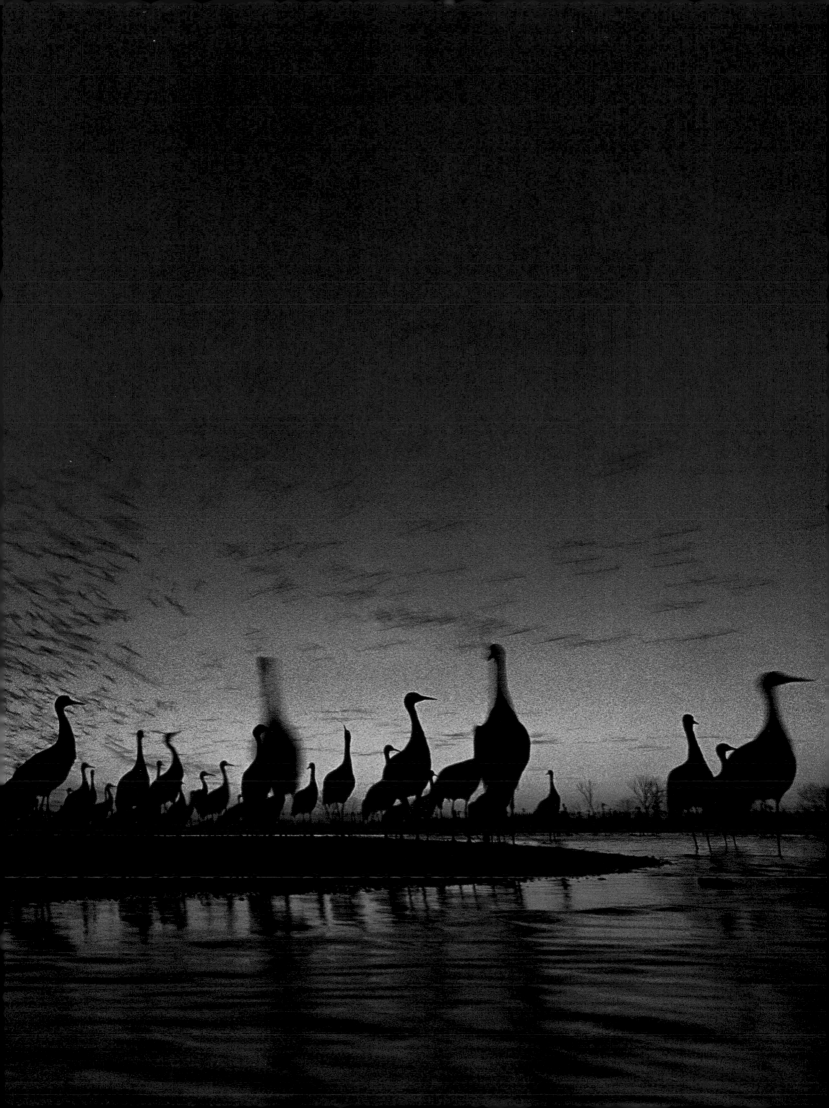

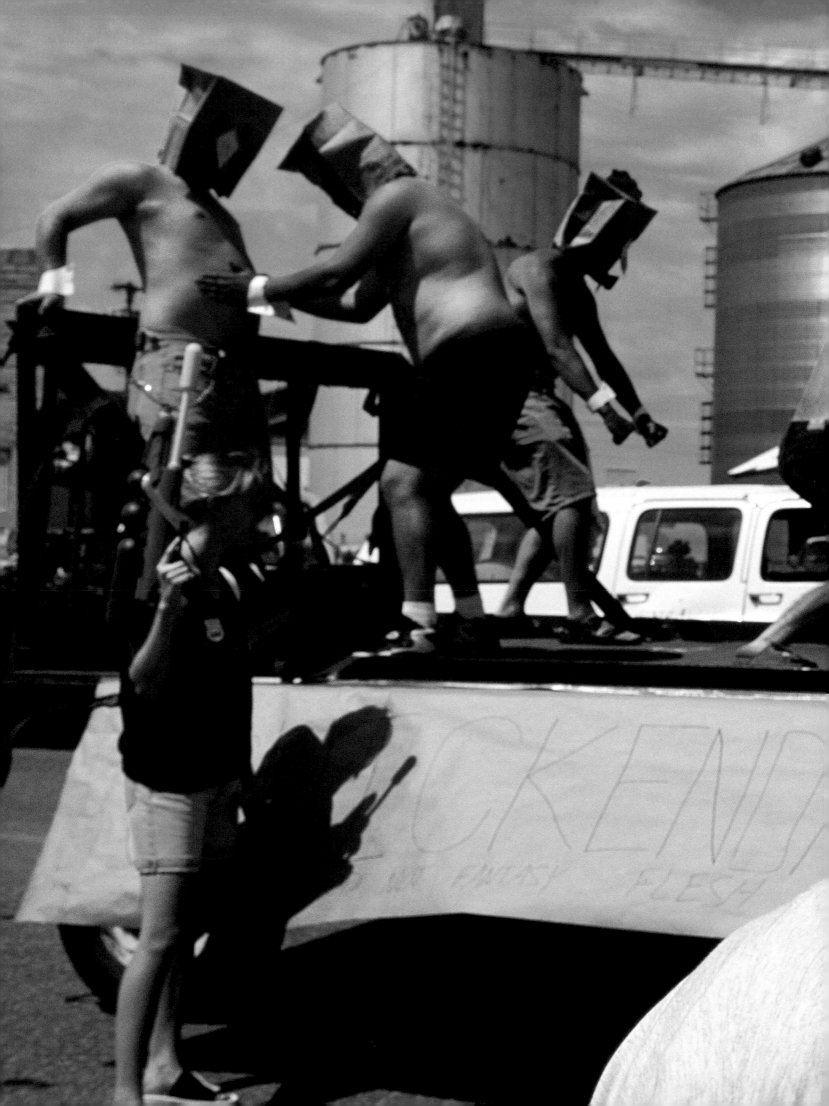

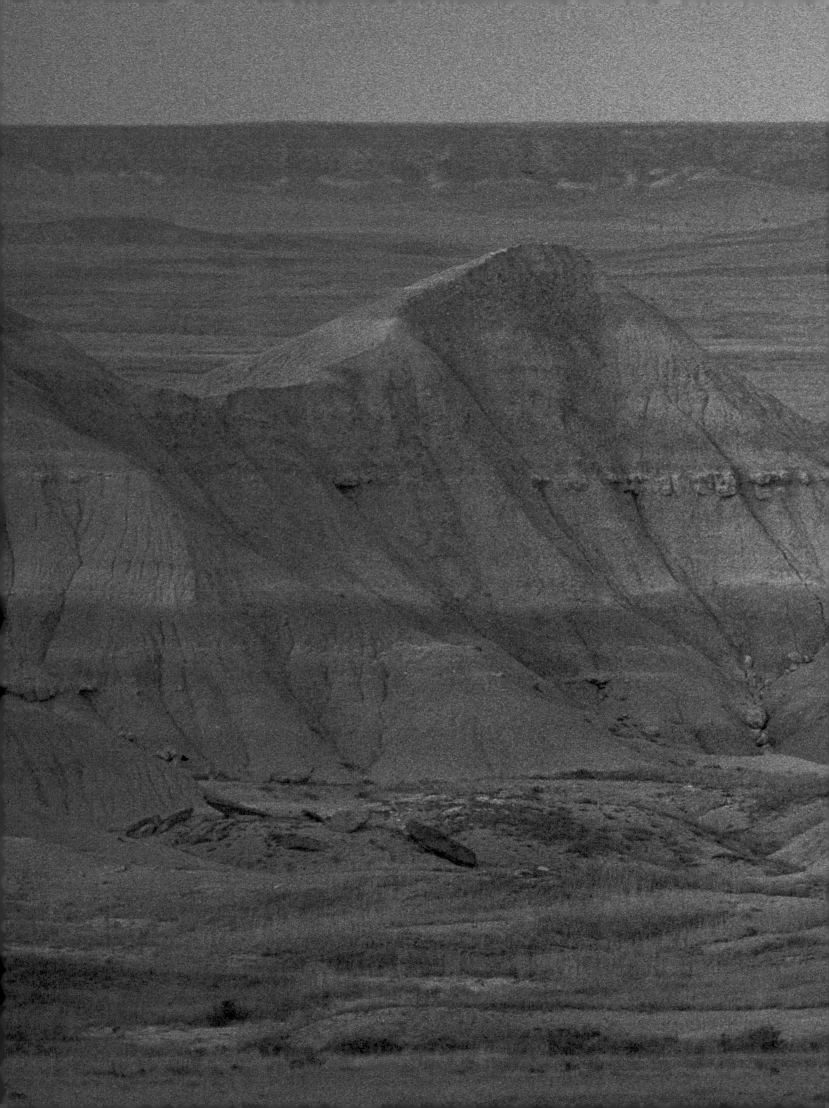

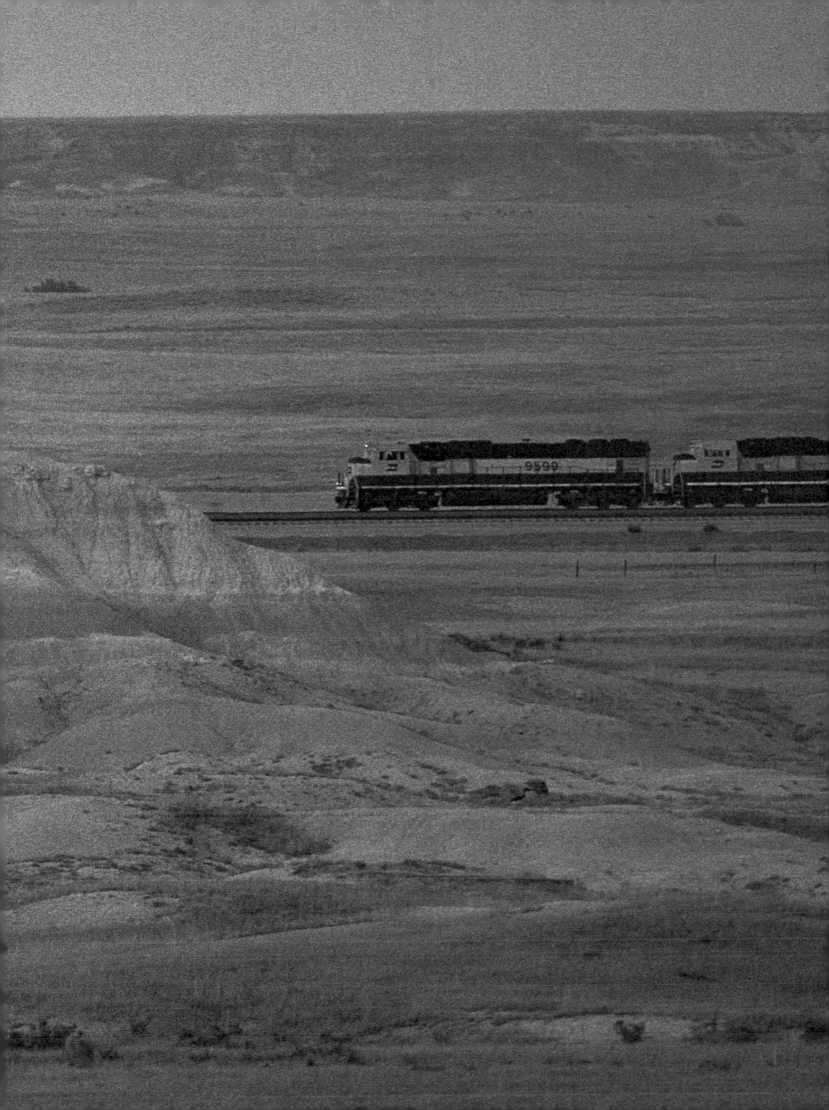

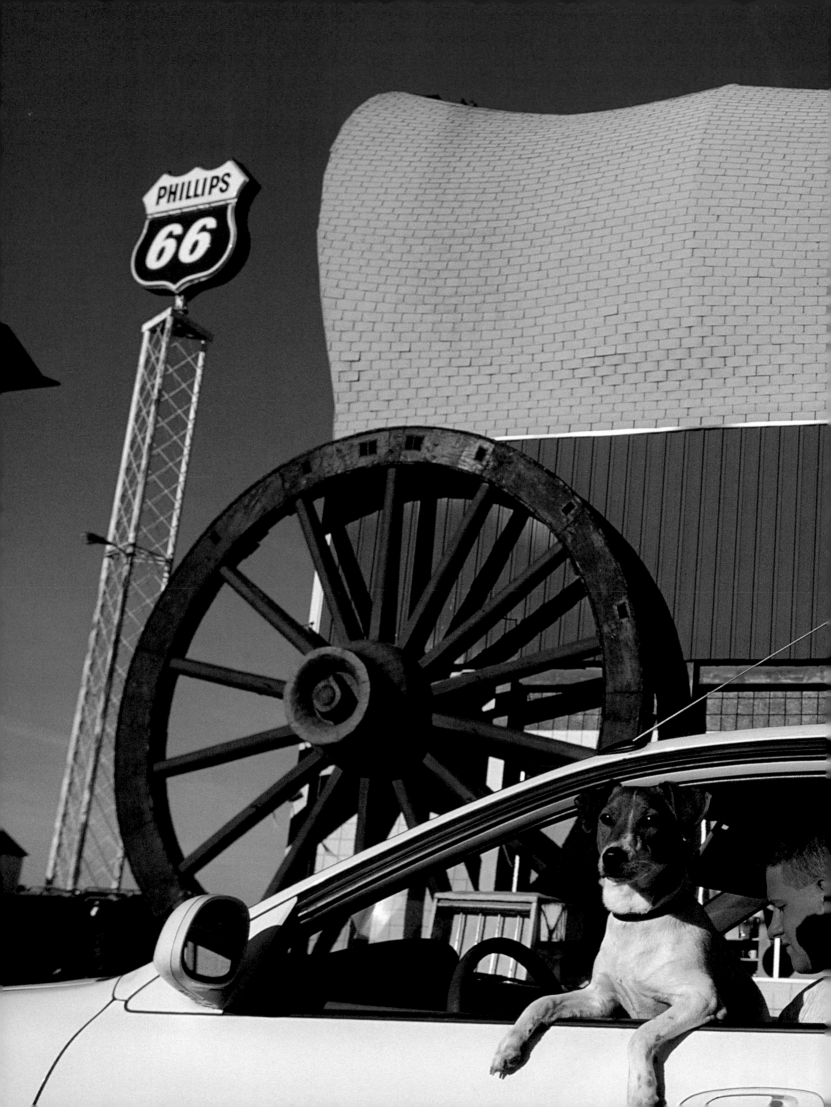

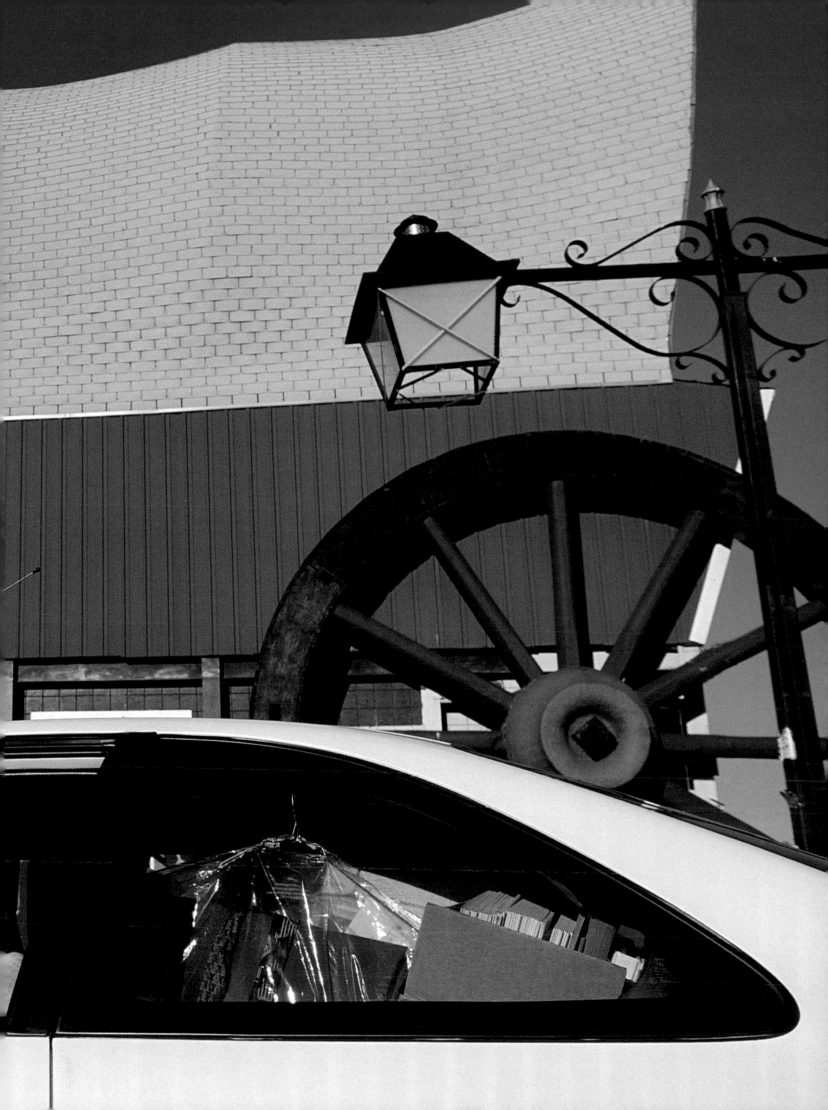

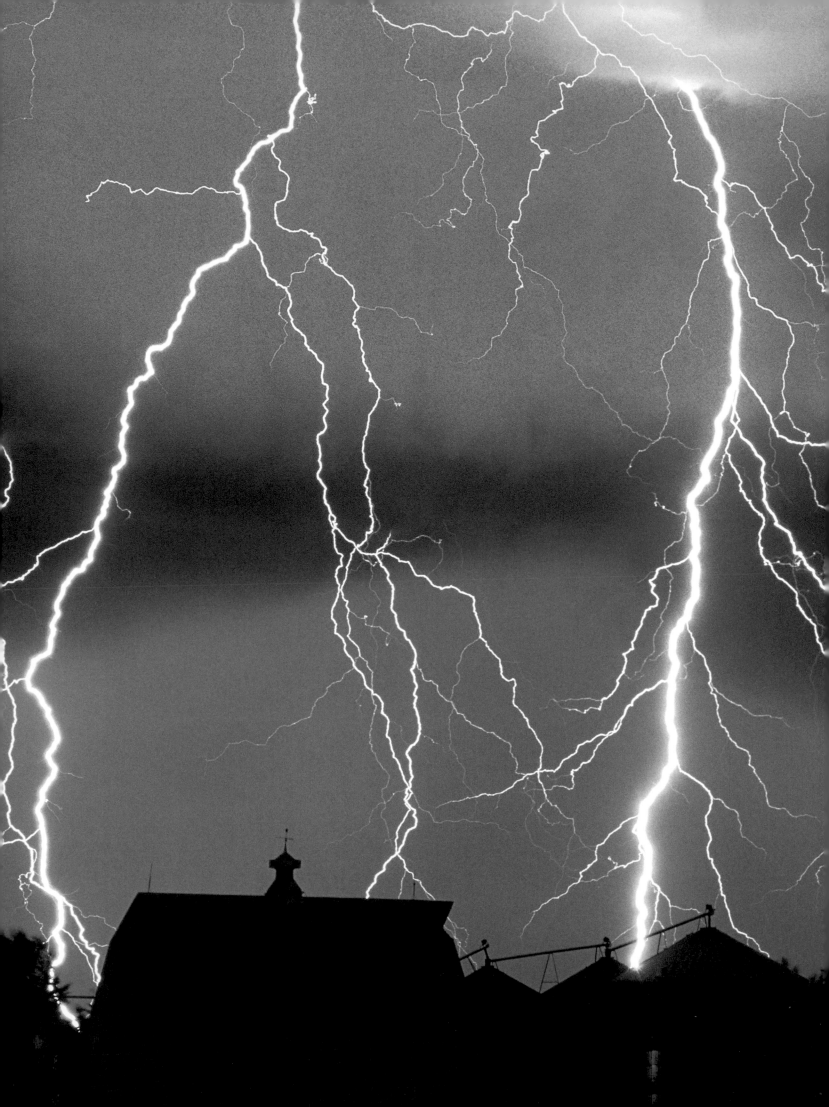

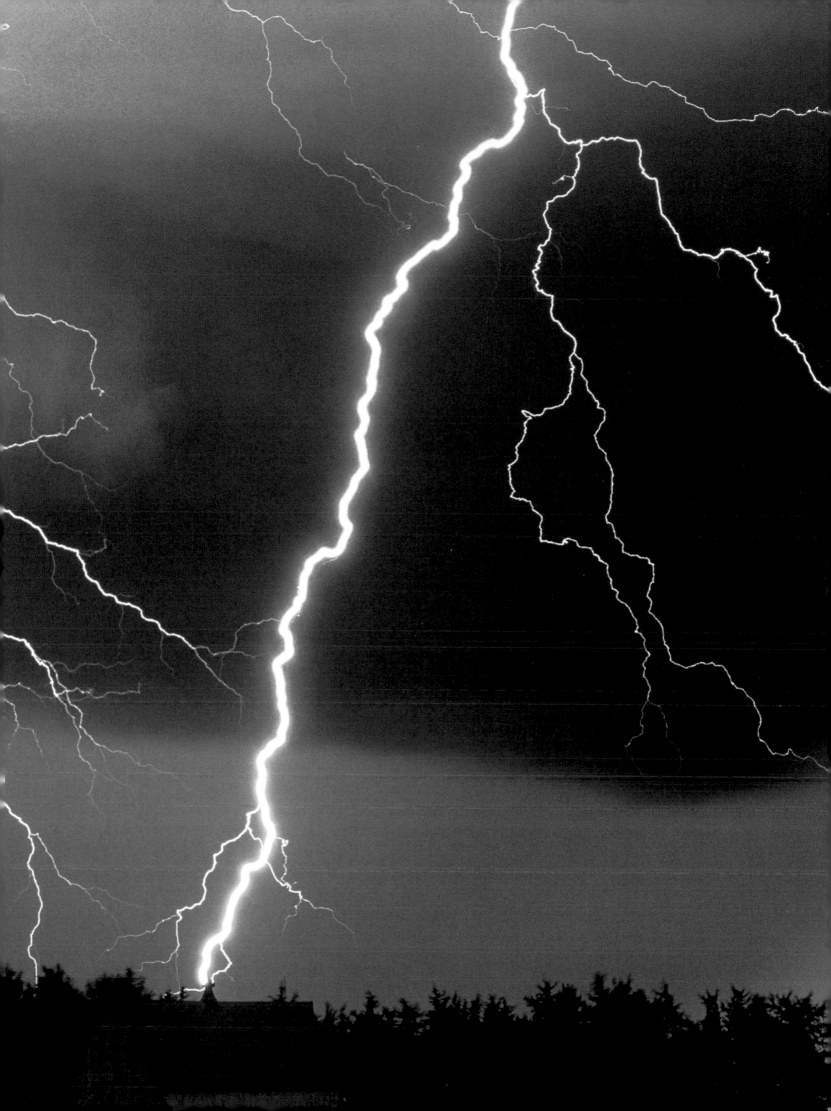

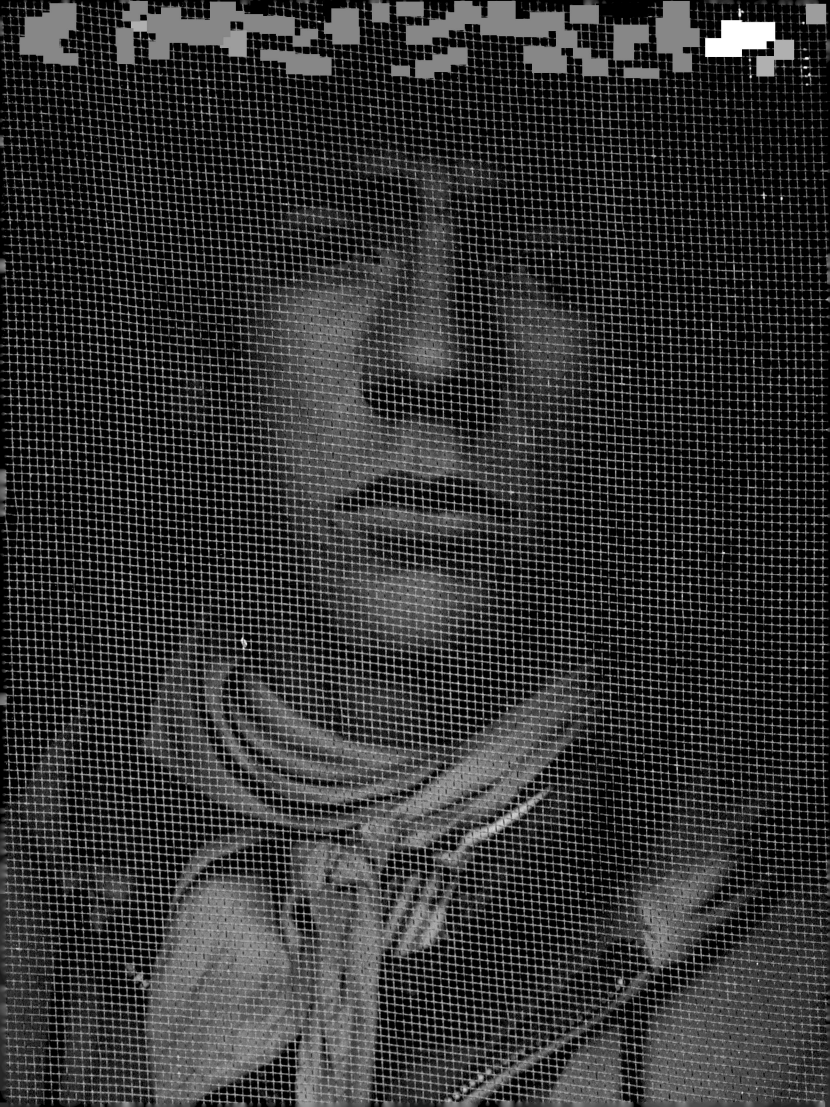

I like the fact that it seems like 1958 here.

That's very comforting to me, and I want it to stay that way.

VIEW OVER A B-2

(*pages 12-13*)

It took two years to line this thing up, calling the military constantly to get permission to go along on a refueling flight. I called the air base here. Then I called the wing command for the bombers in Missouri. Then I called every government bureaucrat on God's green earth. I mean, I've never had such trouble getting permission to do anything. Getting girls to make out with me in high school was easier.

BROTHERLY LUNCH

(*pages 14-15*)

I actually called around to county extension agents to find twin farm boys or girls. I had to do a good picture of farming, and I figured that twins would improve my odds. I'm not that good at photographing farming, but I am shameless. The more smoke and mirrors, the better. So I shot these twins during wheat harvest and hung around with them for a couple of days, and the picture that we actually ended up using is of them eating sandwiches at the local cafe. Nothing of the twins actually farming ever made it

into print. I think the reason this picture made it into *National Geographic* is that one of the main editors back there really likes chicken-fried steak sandwiches.

SANDHILL CRANES

(*pages 16-17*)

This was shot using a remote camera that was buried in a sand bar in the Platte River. Thousands of birds coming in each evening was something I wanted to convey. They remind me a little bit of the scene in *The Wizard of Oz* where the witch sends all those flying monkeys out into the night sky to collect Dorothy. To avoid spooking the birds, I had to leave the camera in the sandbar overnight. Since rivers tend to rise once in awhile, I worried that the camera would be gone by morning. Things worked out fine, but I didn't mention this to the guy that lent me the gear.

CHICKEN FESTIVAL

(*pages 18-19*)

The Wayne Chicken Show is three days of nothing but chicken puns, fried chicken, eggs and, of course, the Chick-endale dancers. These are a bunch of fraternity boys who strap on bow ties, put chicken bags over their heads and become an overweight version of the Chippendales. They go through the town on a float with things written all over their bodies like "Will peck for food."

BADLANDS

(*pages 20-21*)

The northwest corner of Nebraska is the start of the Badlands, believe it or not. Mostly it's an empty place. The only sounds you hear are coal trains running day and night across the "fruited plains." Of course, there's not too much fruit up there; it's just rock and shortgrass prairie.

COVERED WAGON

(*pages 22-23*)

Another hint of the Old West is in Milford. This is supposed to lure tourists off the interstate. I don't think it works. I suggested to the clerk that they erect a 300-foot-tall ear of corn. Then they'd really have some-

thing! The clerk wouldn't even fake a smile for me. He's heard every oversized joke on the planet, and I was only rubbing salt in the wound.

LIGHTNING

(*pages 24-25*)

Lightning really rattles my cage. It can get you killed out on the plains, and this storm looked awful coming into our farm near Walton. This is a 15-second time exposure—the longest 15 seconds of my life, I might add.

COWBOY

(*facing page*)

I shot 125 rolls of ranching pictures out in the Sandhills, and this is the only one that was published, one frame of a young cowboy named Mark Vinton. That's all we used. I like it because it kind of looks like a painting. Photographers always want to be painters, and screens are good for that— one more smoke and mirrors trick I've come to rely on over the years.

We have guys in big hats

being thrown high in the air

off a variety of big animals.

Now *that's* good photography.

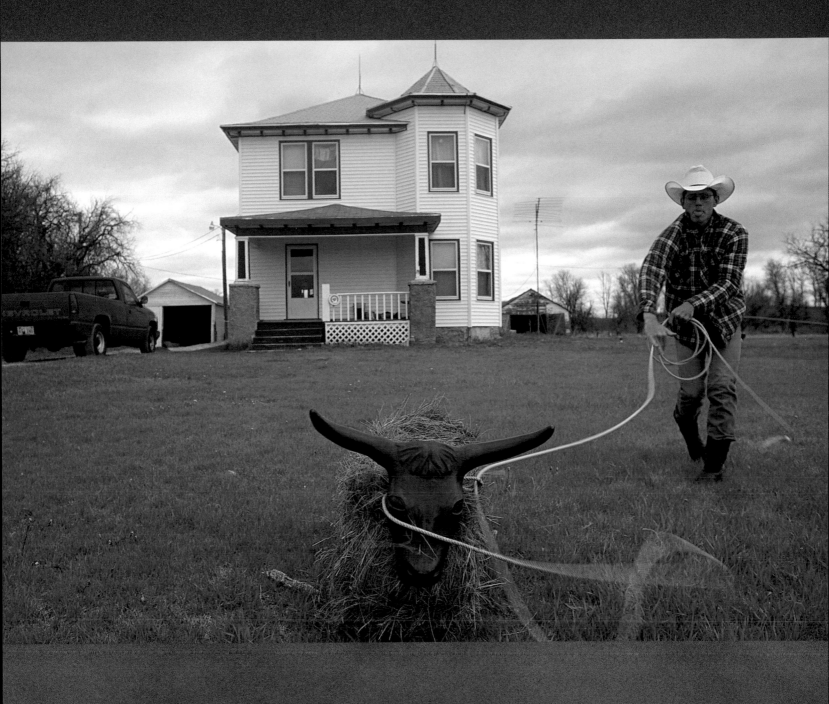

PLASTIC STEER ROPING, STAPLETON

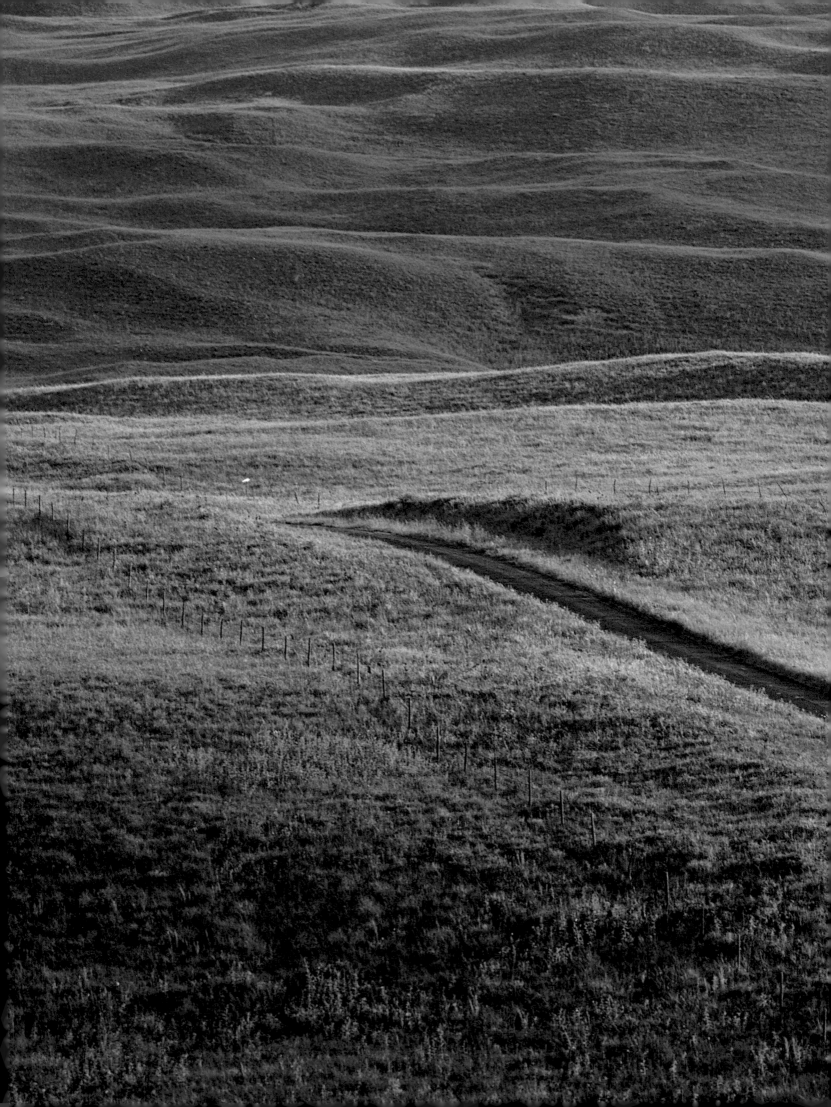

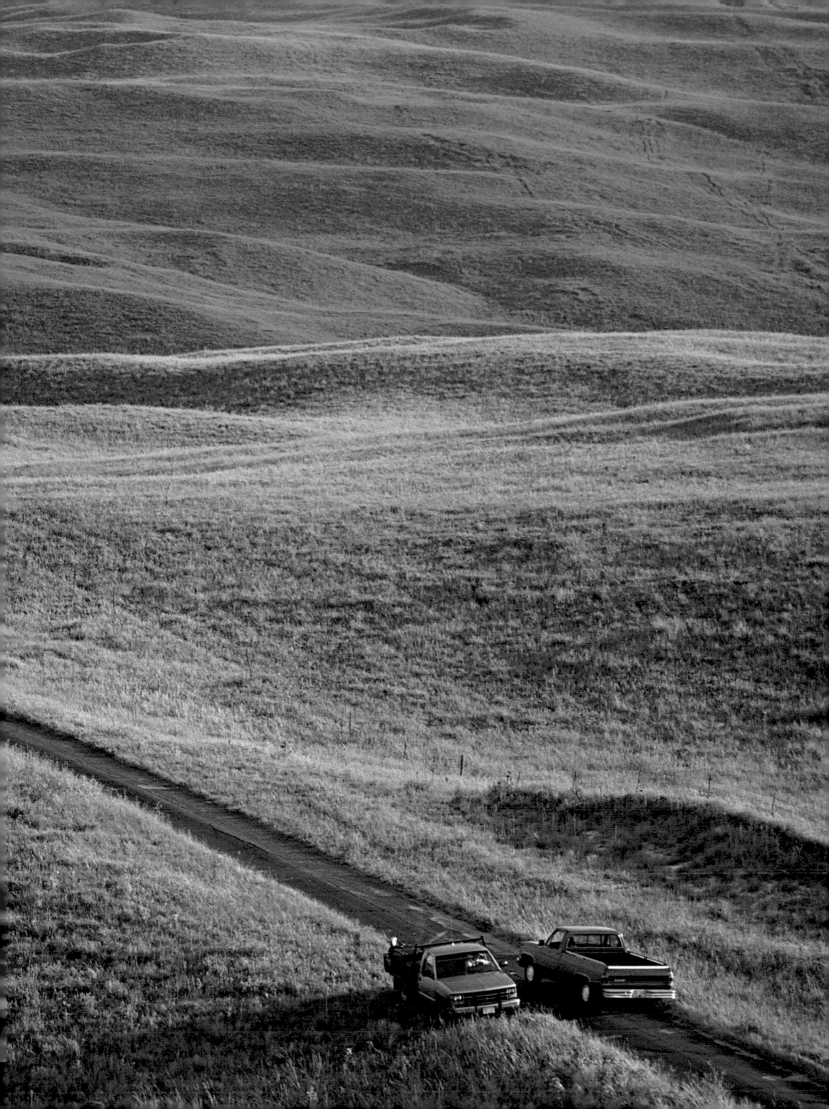

◀ *(pages 30-31)* Rancher Hop Vinton has an airplane. He flew me around the Sandhills so we could do some aerials, and all he'd let me pay him was gas money. He wouldn't take a dime more. This scene is very typical out there, with undulating, grass-covered sand dunes stretching for miles. Cows far out-number people. If you see another truck, you often pull over and talk, which is probably not much different from when the pioneers were headed out in covered wagons. You don't see a whole lot of people out there, so if you have the time to talk, you pull over and chat a little bit. This is only a one-lane road, by the way. You hold your breath going over the hills because you never know what's going to be on the other side. Car wrecks are a leading cause of early death out here.

▶ I like my job on days like this. I was given a horse of my own and actually got to help on a cattle roundup. I felt just like Billy Crystal in *City Slickers*. Even from the back of a moving horse it's hard to take a lousy picture out here. Every thing is clean. Photographers love clean backgrounds. Then you just fill your frame with cattle and cowboys. The windmills only add to the feeling of the Old West.

32

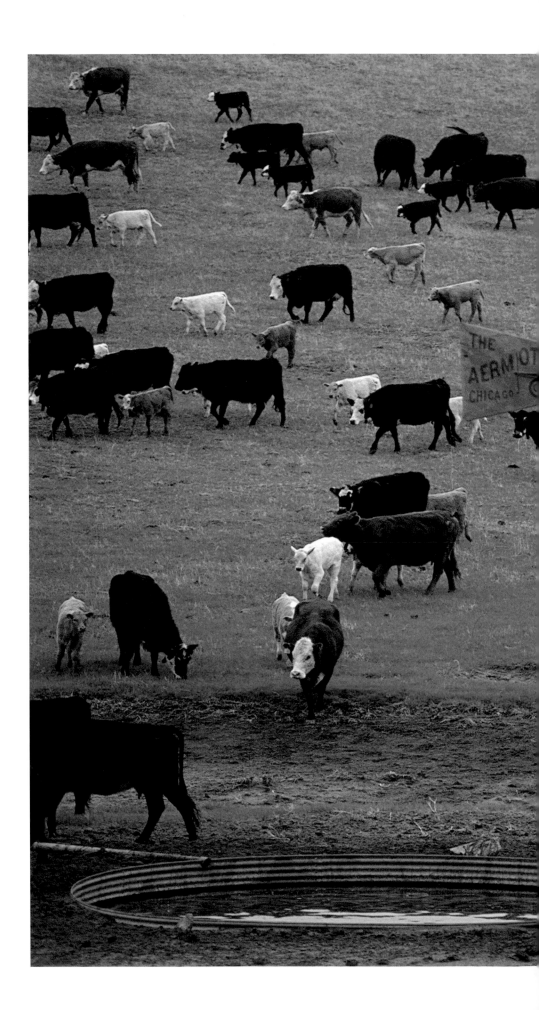

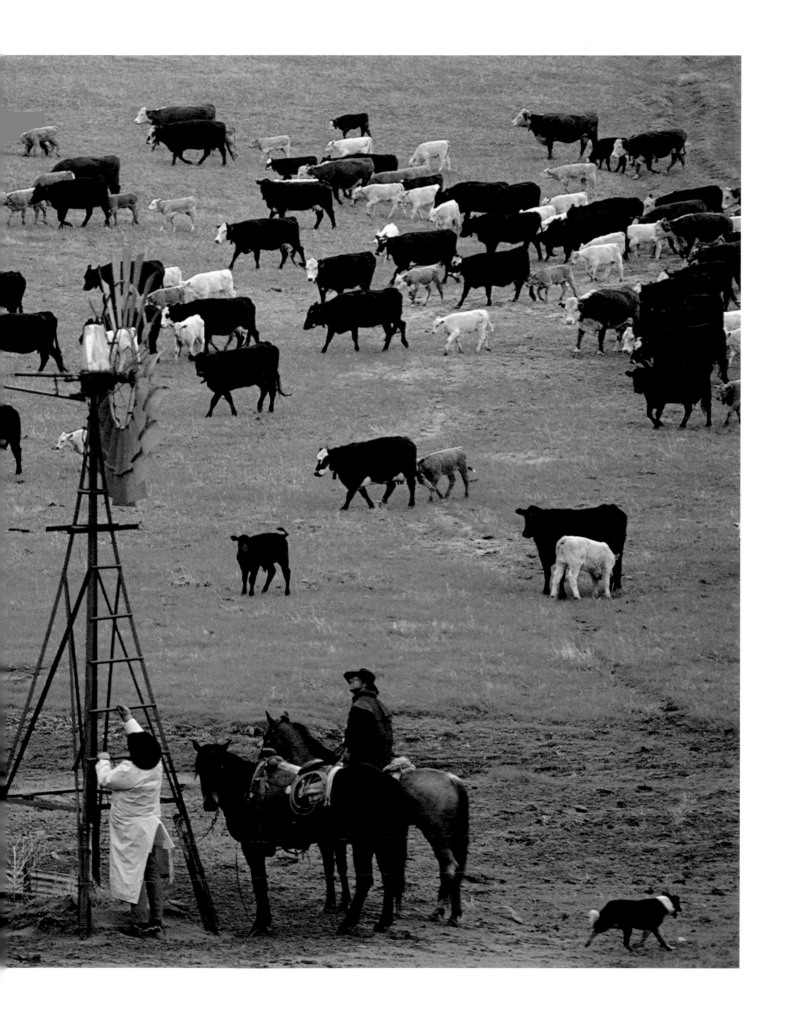

This is Hop Vinton's brother Chris riding
a horse as fast as he can to catch up
with a stray cow. We call it "panned"
action in the business. I imagine Chris
just calls it too damned blurry to tell
what's going on. I stayed in a one-room
schoolhouse on his ranch. There were
holes in the screens and plenty of
mosquitoes. I woke up looking like
I had chicken pox. Chris thought that
was funny.

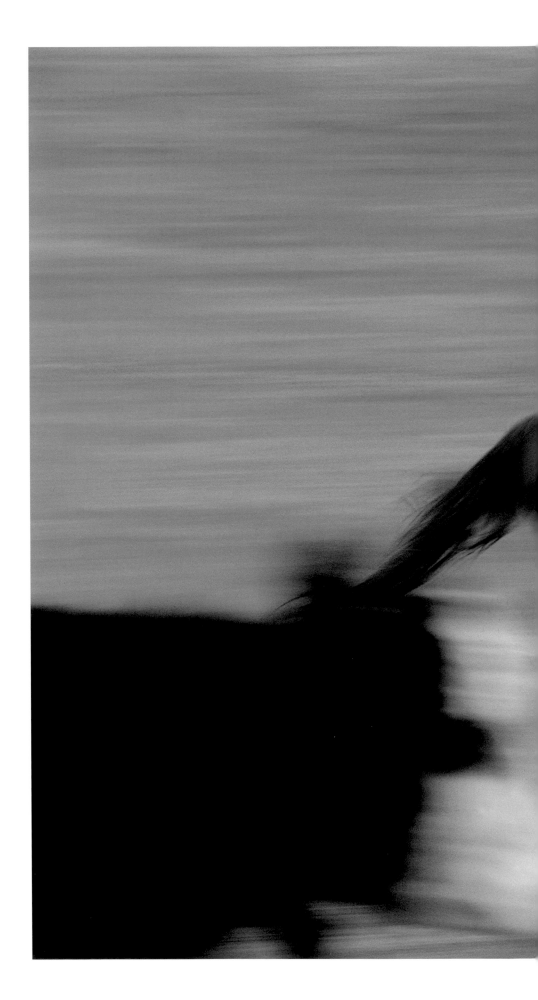

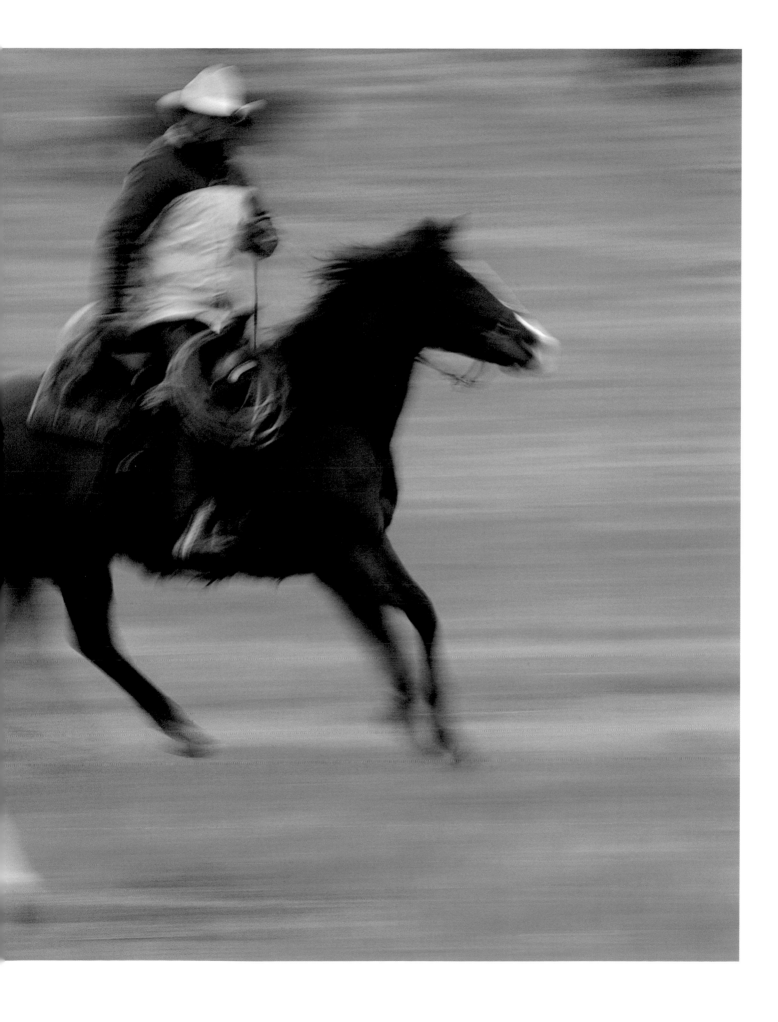

Blood, mud and the smell of burning flesh — that's branding time. It's confusing to a non-cowboy like me. All I could do was hug the fence. They can get one calf done in about a minute, so if you're in the wrong place at the wrong time, they'll brand you! You really have to watch your step. Actually, while I was out there, one guy did get partially branded on his thigh. He let out kind of a yelp.

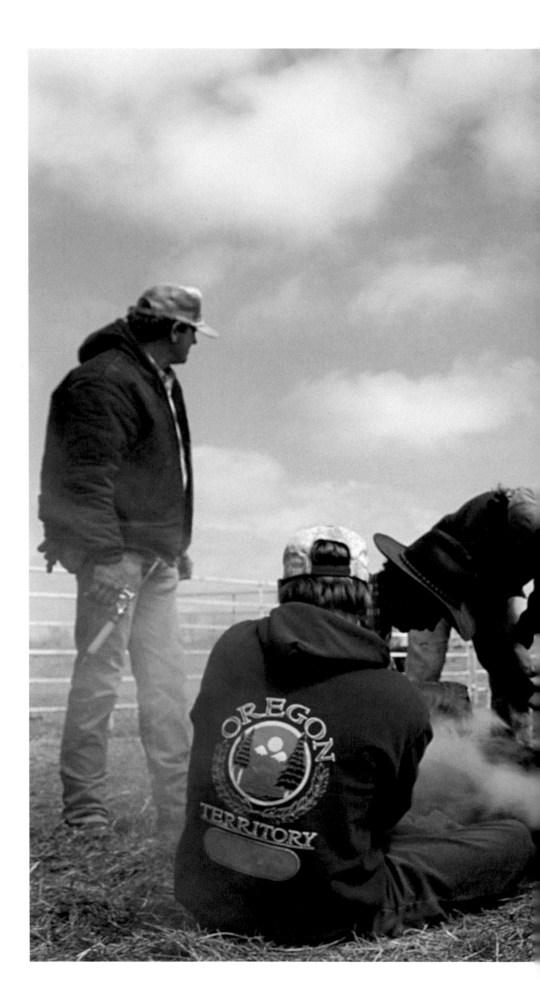

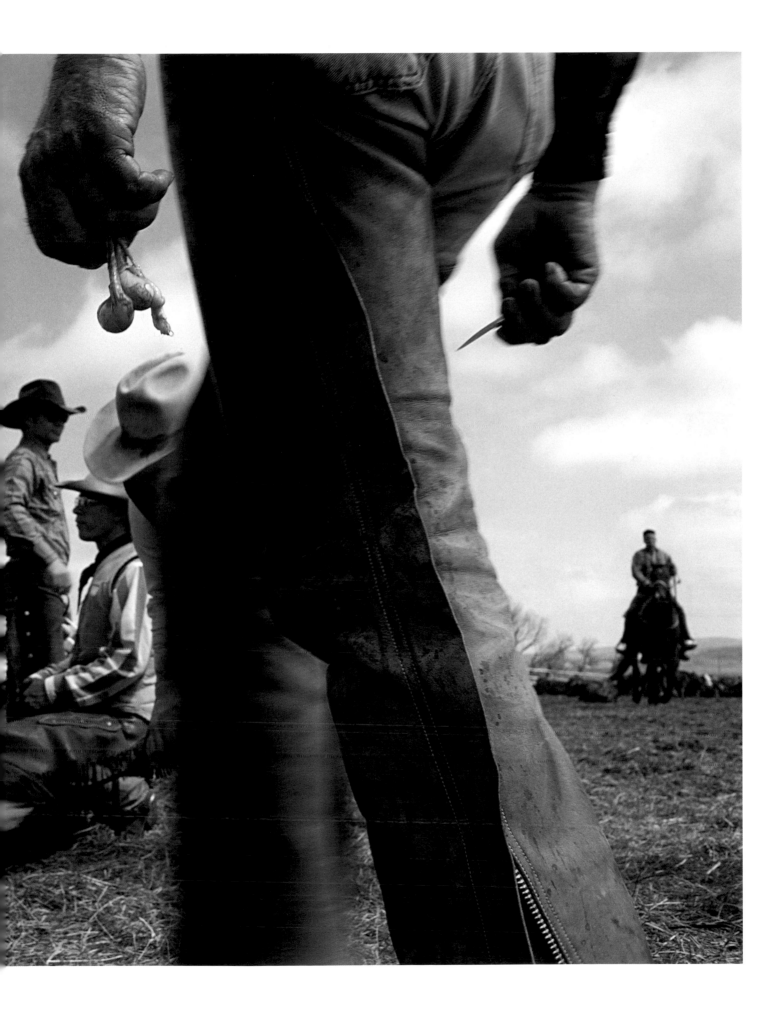

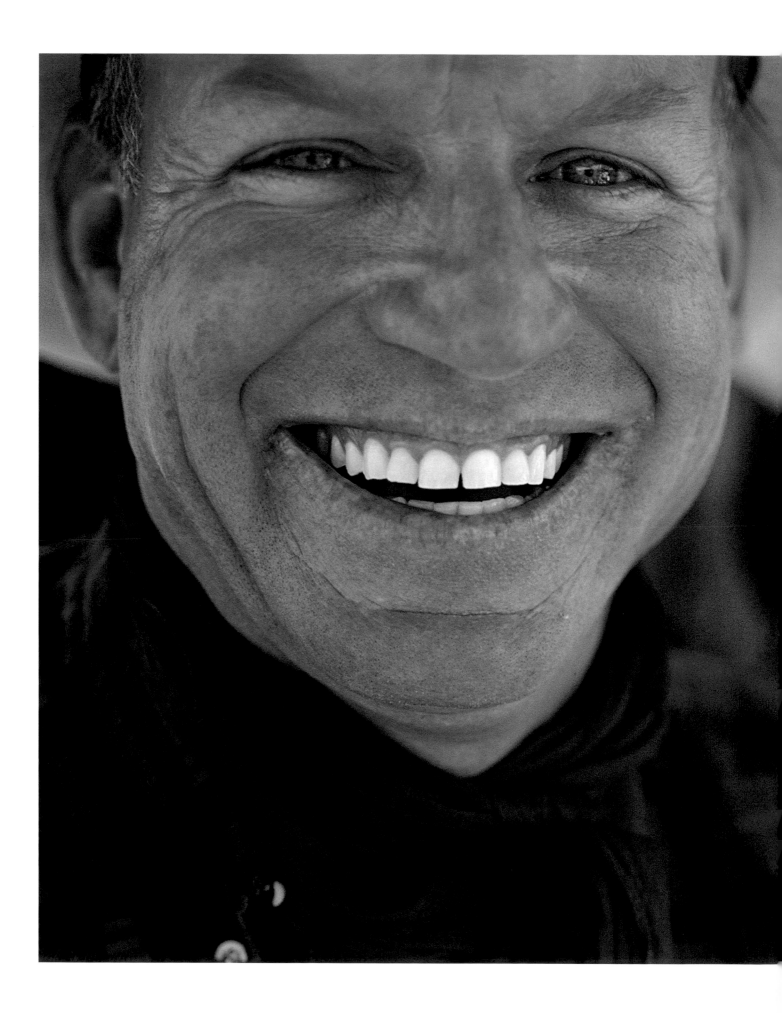

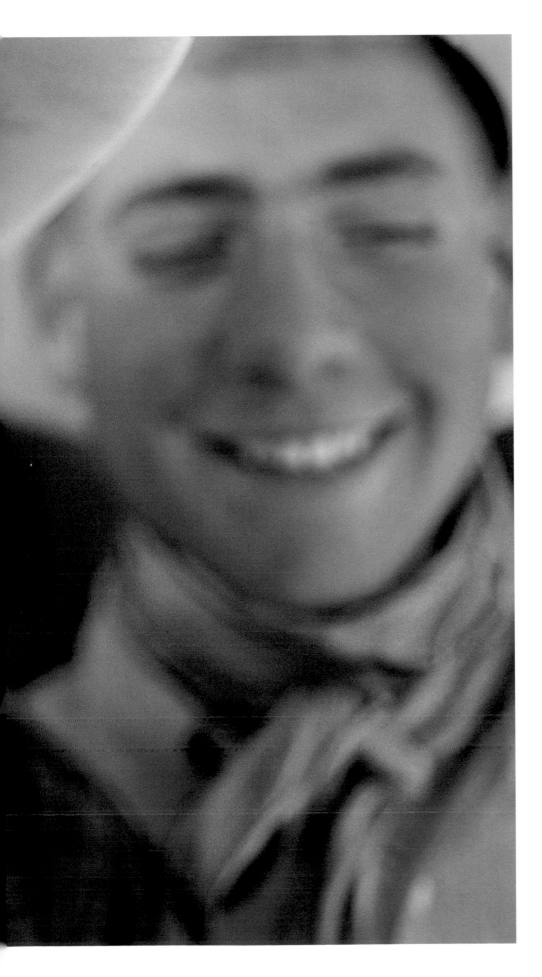

This is Hop Vinton and his son Mark. Hop's got good teeth. I don't think he chews tobacco.

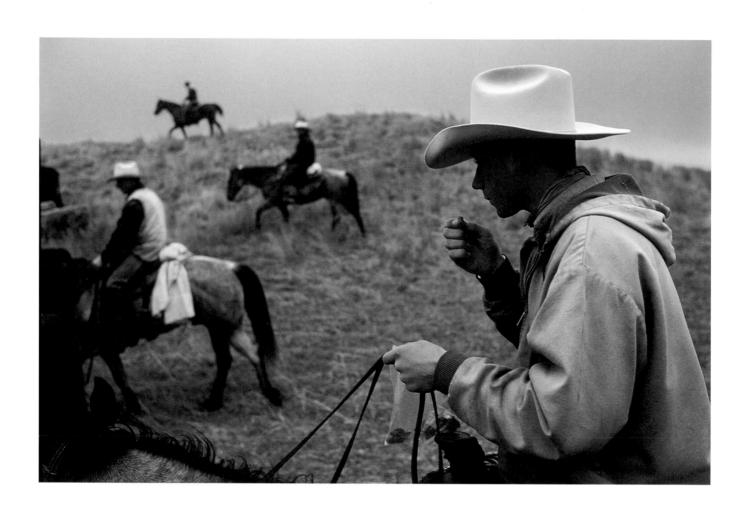

40   Mark Vinton, the kid you saw through the screen door, helps round up the cattle. No more
      hard tack and whiskey; it's gummy bears that are the critical component of any cattle drive.

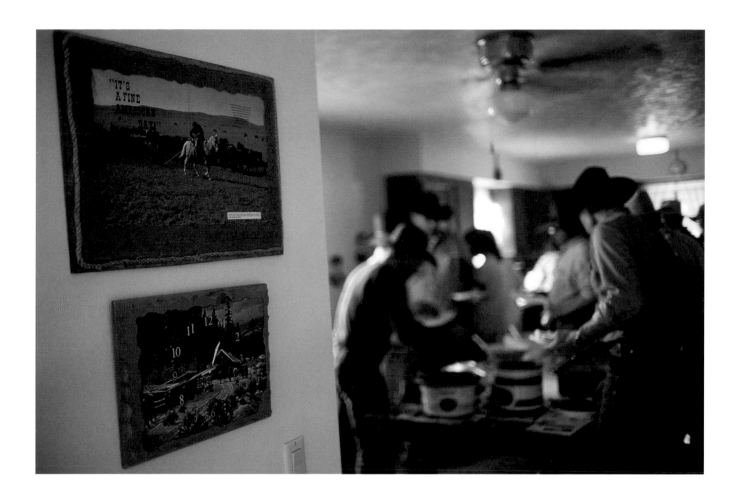

Perhaps one of the most critical aspects of working cattle is lunch. In fact, these guys will start working at four in the morning just to be done by lunchtime. They call this meal either dinner or supper. I can never keep that straight. Anyway, it's often a potluck, with beef cooked a dozen ways and various vegetable dishes containing Miracle Whip. One wife spelled out a favorite for me, the seven-layer salad. "Starting at the bottom, you want your chopped lettuce, celery, peppers, onions, frozen peas, sugar, and about a quart of Miracle Whip. Spread that Miracle Whip clear to the edges to keep the air out. You don't want your vegetables going limp. Sprinkle the top with shredded cheddar cheese and bacon bits. But you don't want your cheese too thick. You don't want to overpower the Miracle Whip. The cheese is just a garnish. Remember that."

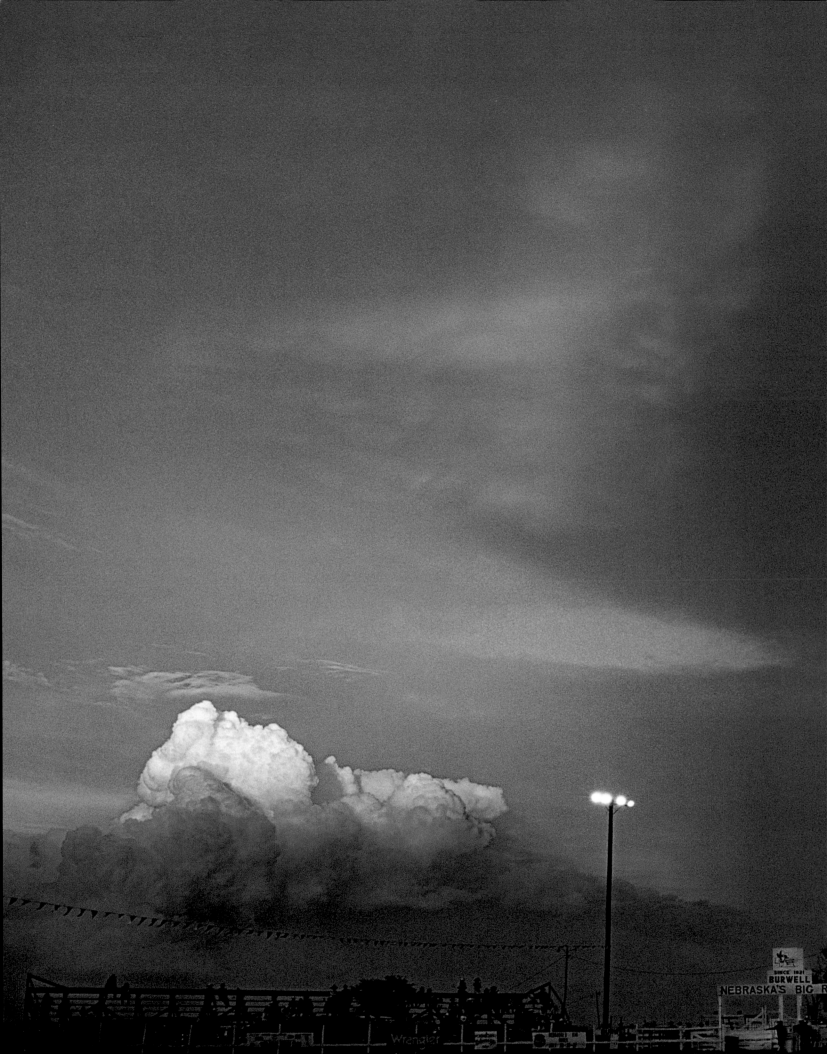

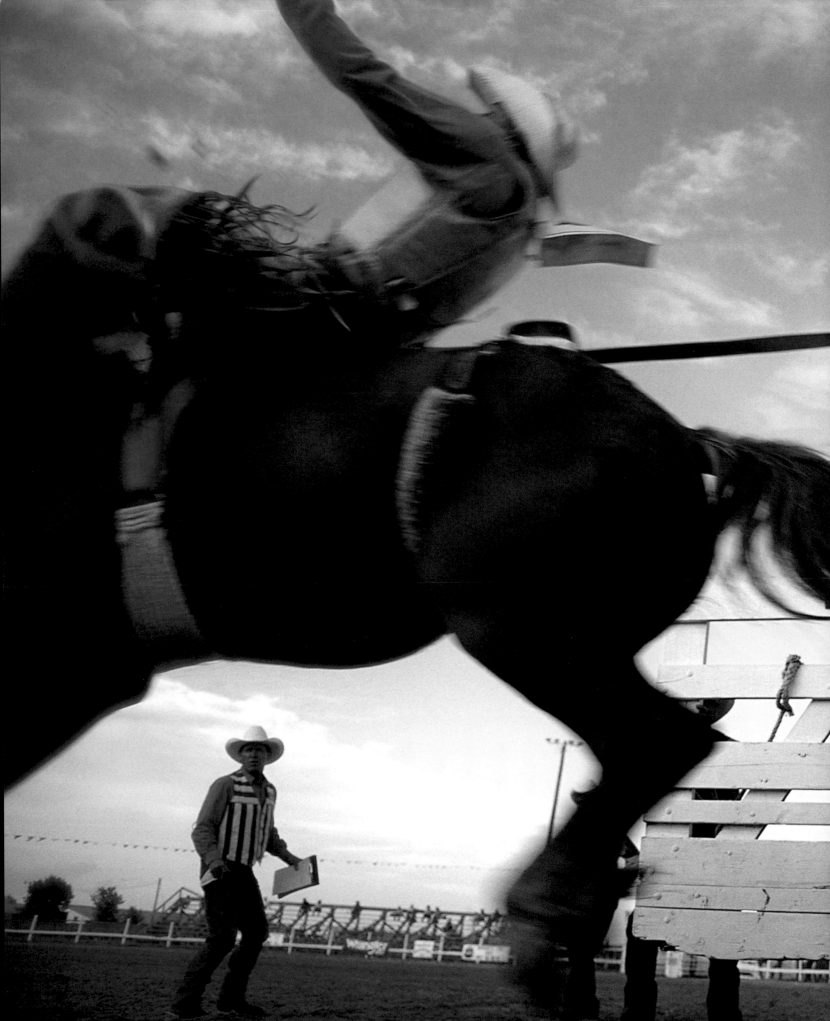

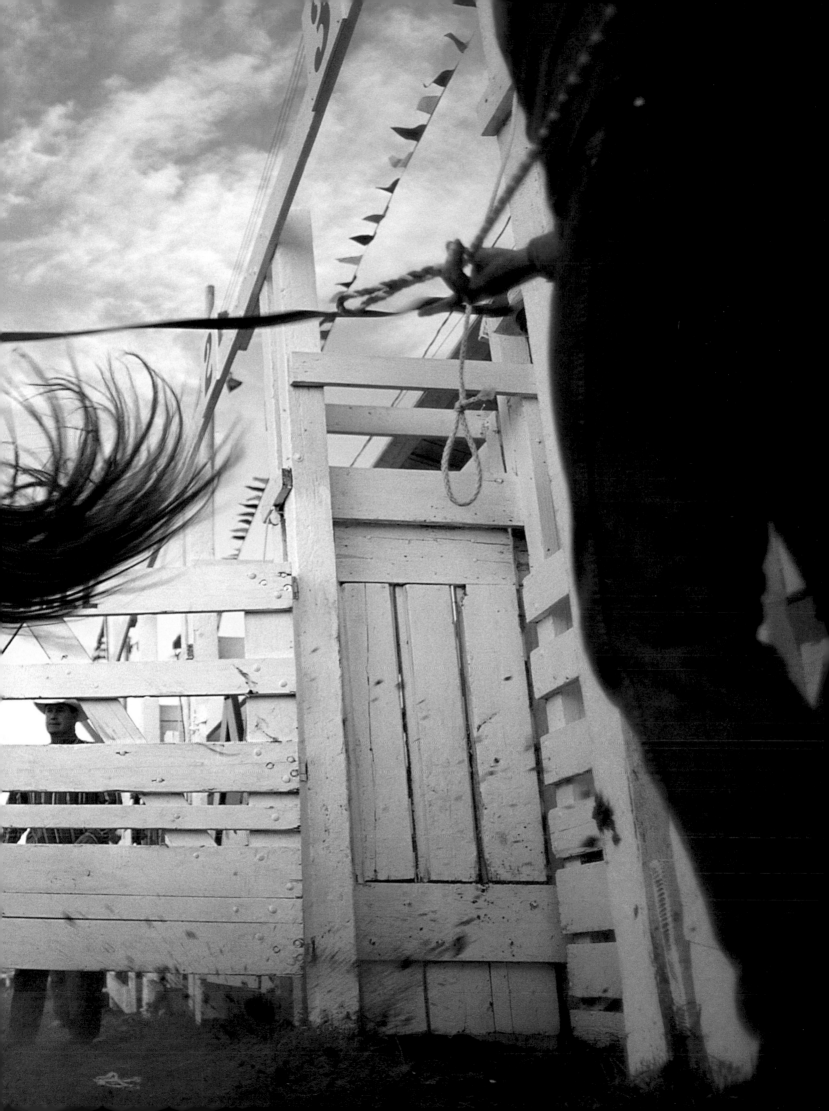

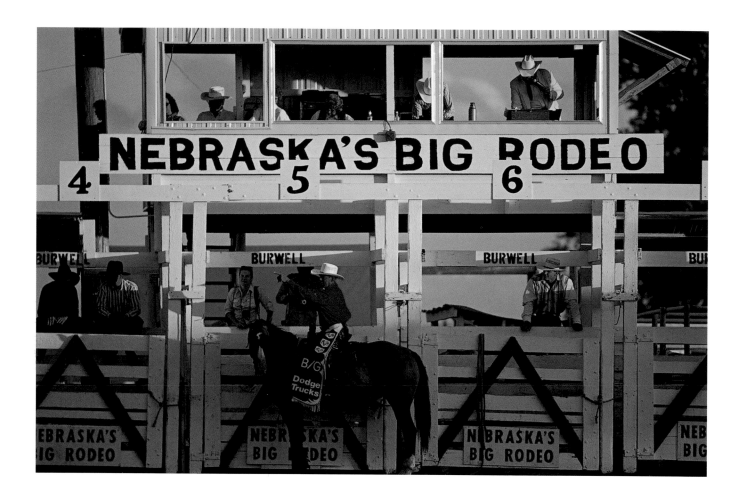

◀ *(pages 42-43)* With all that ranching, it's no wonder that Nebraska was the state that invented the rodeo. Buffalo Bill's Wild West Show in North Platte was the first, they say. As if rodeos aren't wild enough, this night featured the sky splitting in half between light and dark. I heard a cowboy behind me look up and say, "Well, I'll be dipped!" The man standing on the horse on top of the trailer is the One-Armed Bandit. He was the half-time show. A former lineman for a power company, he got out of the business after nearly being electrocuted and losing an arm. Now he makes his living going to rodeos and driving a herd of horses up on the top of his trailer. He stands on the back of his horse, raises his hat and salutes the crowd.

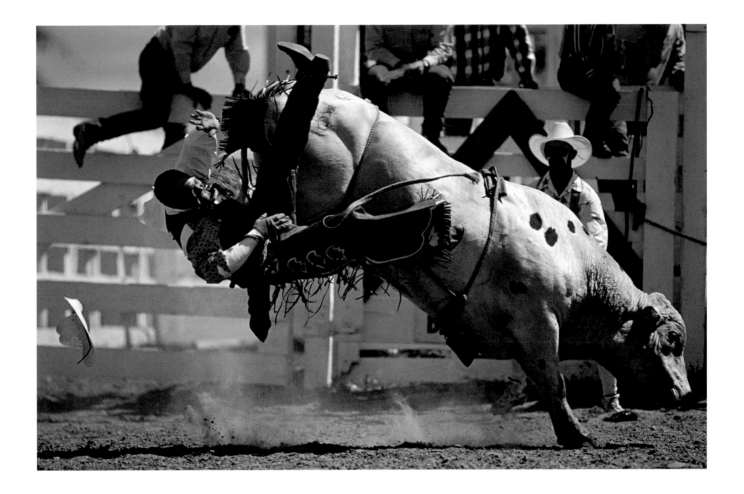

▲ I liked Nebraska's Big Rodeo at Burwell. Even when these guys have a successful ride, they're all torn up. Successful means you stayed on the critter for eight seconds. That's plenty of time to cause permanent back problems. There was a chiropractor on duty behind the stands, straightening spines *before* the ride. Those who could walk afterwards also sought his attention. "There's a pot of prize money to split," one aching rider told me, "enough to pay the hospital bill, and that's it." There are no old bull riders from what I can tell.

I met this guy in the Wagon Wheel Bar
the night before the rodeo. He wanted
to show off his badge of honor, the
missing teeth created by an errant hoof
in a previous year's wild horse race.
They give a big shiny belt buckle to the
cowboy that finishes the race first, if
there are any finishers. He really wanted
the belt buckle. He tried his luck again
the next day, and I photographed him
getting his shoulder dislocated.

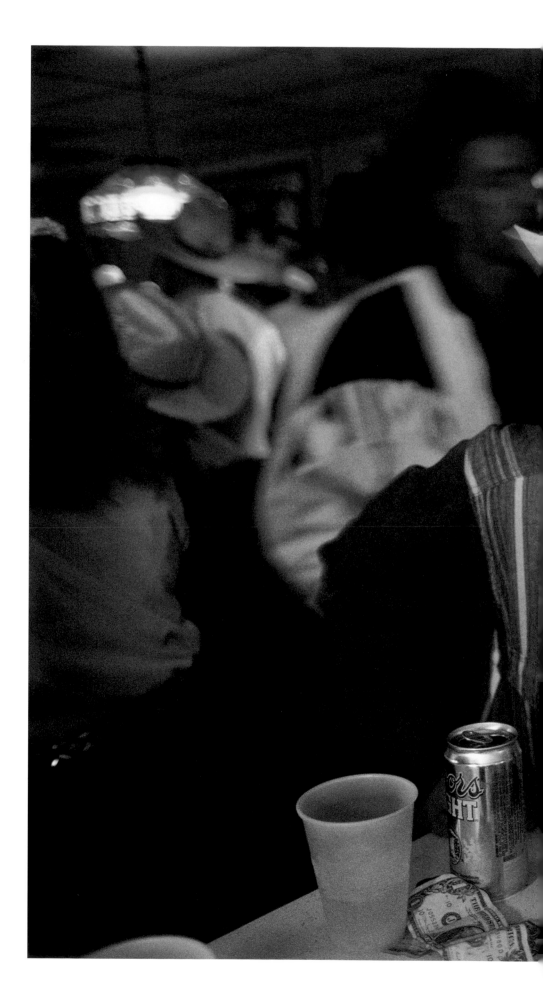

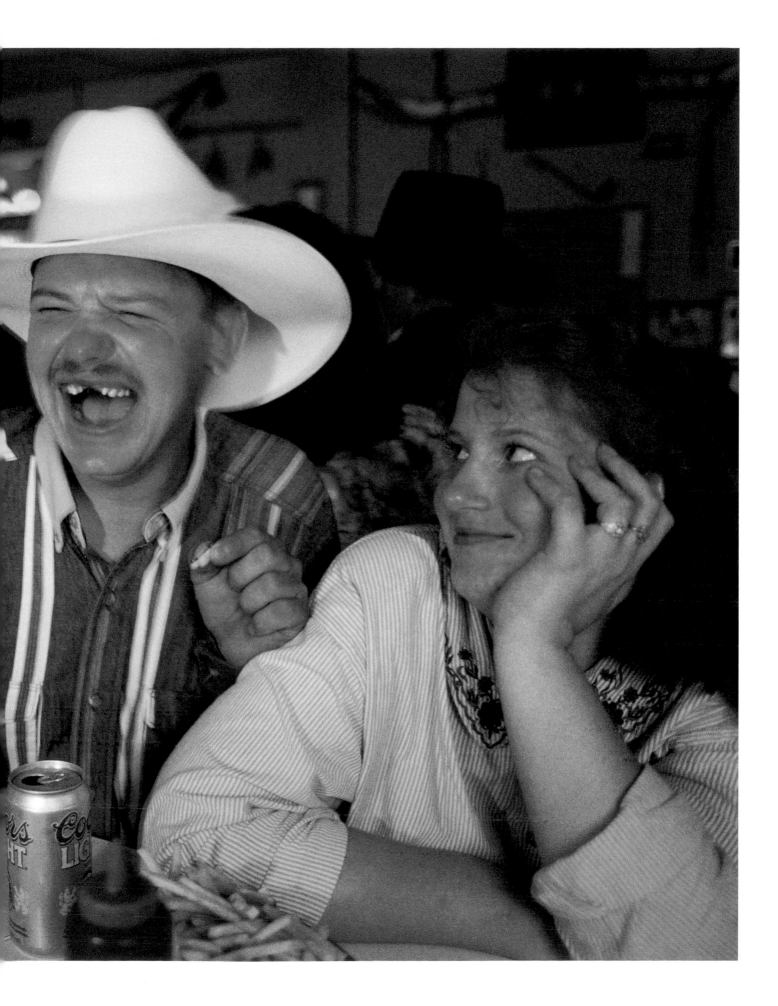

Give me your trivial,

your frivolous, your trite.

That's what I'm after.

And when something subtle

happens and it makes for a

keeper picture, I'm astounded.

I guess even a blind cat

catches a mouse once in awhile.

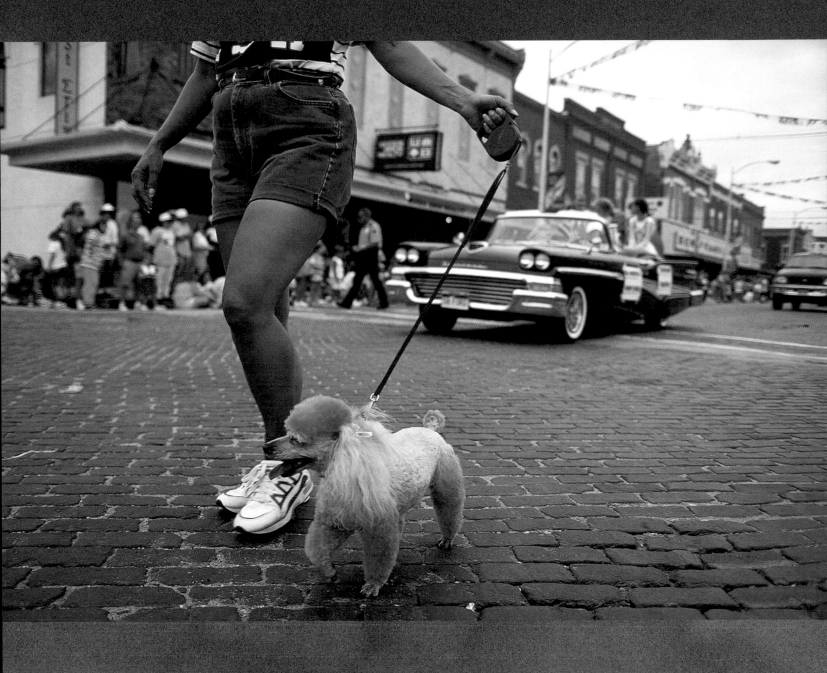

JULY FOURTH PARADE, SEWARD

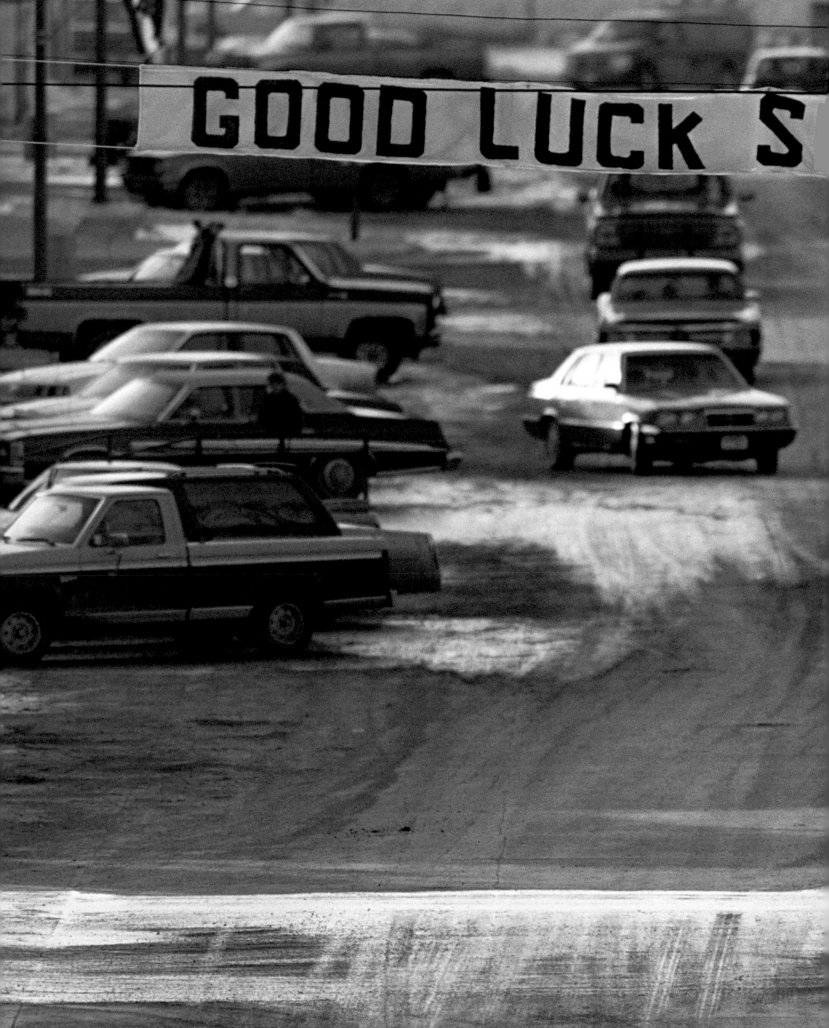

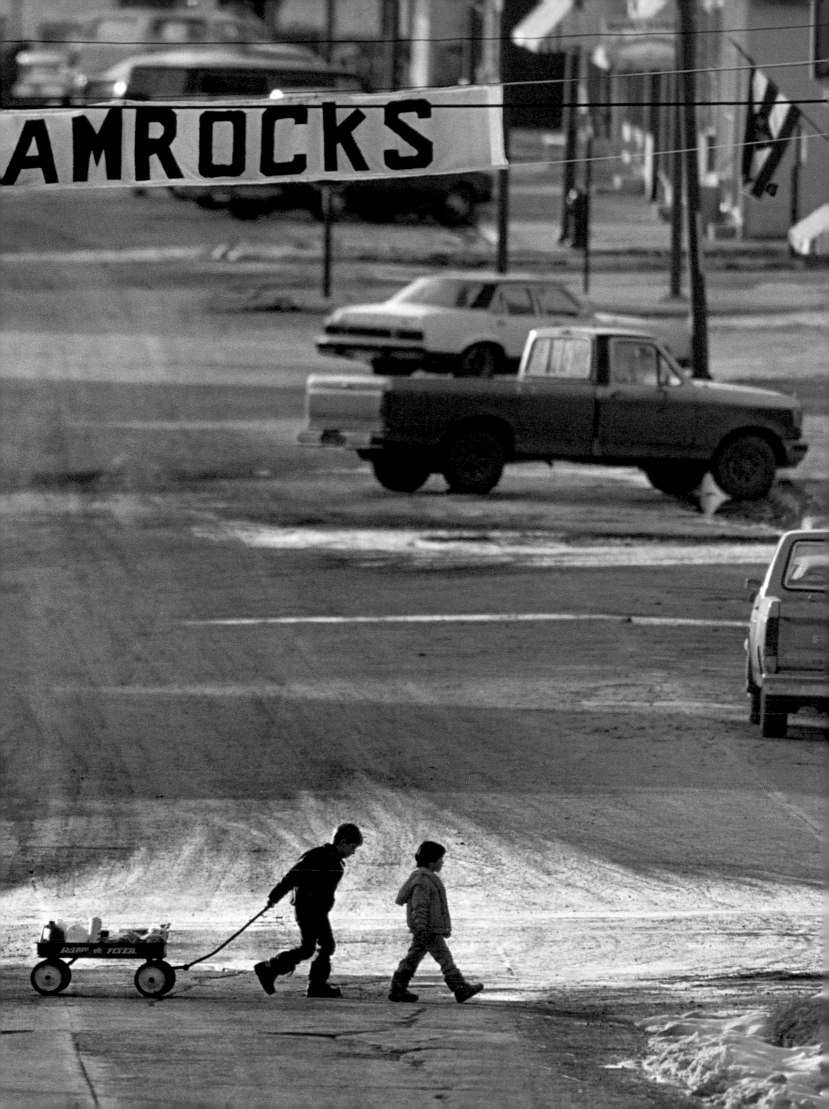

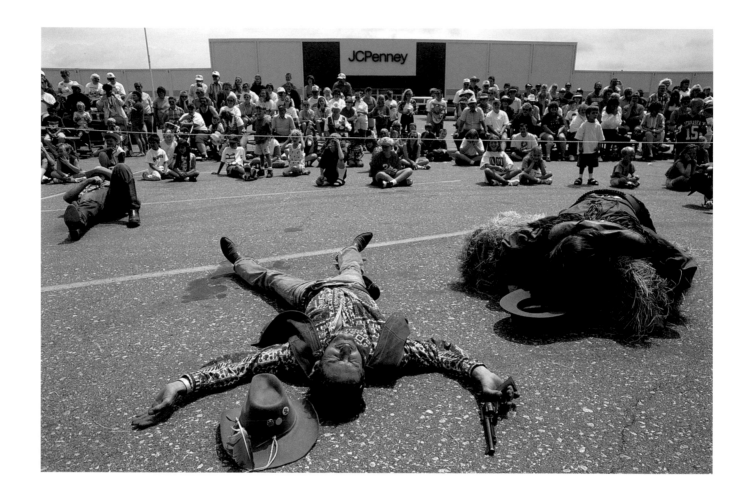

54 ◄ *(pages 52-53)* How many places do you know of in the U.S. where you can send your kids to the store by themselves? Spaulding is one such town. Here kids can take their little red wagon and go get groceries. Mom doesn't have to worry about anything except getting her change back.

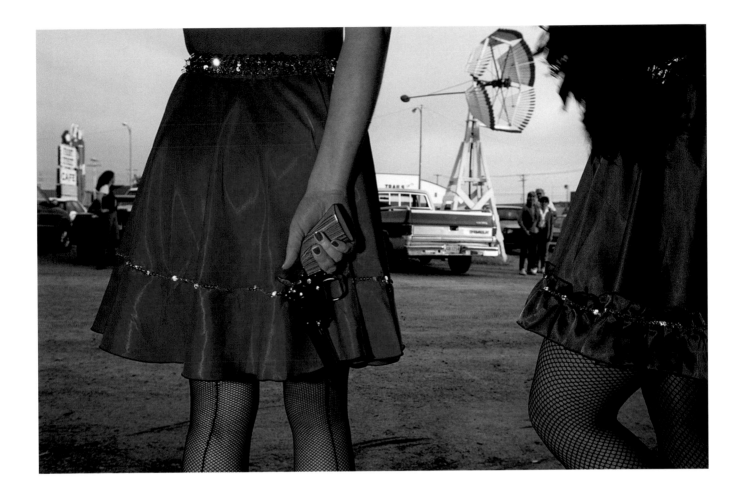

◄ The Old West is alive and well in Nebraska, as is evidenced every summer out in the western end of the state. Tourists these days don't even care where a gunfight is held—or that it's fake. They just want to see grown men pretending to shoot each other and play dead. My wife thinks this picture is lousy because she can't tell what the dead cowboy on the right is wearing. Everybody's a critic. ▲ This is in Ogallala, another historic cow town. During the summer, college kids dressed as saloon girls have a fake gunfight out in the parking lot. Every night at sunset they pretend to gun down one of the members of the theatre company. They hope a dead cowboy lying in their gravel parking lot will draw tourists off the street.

Pancake makeup, big feathers and
access into their dressing room—
need I say more?

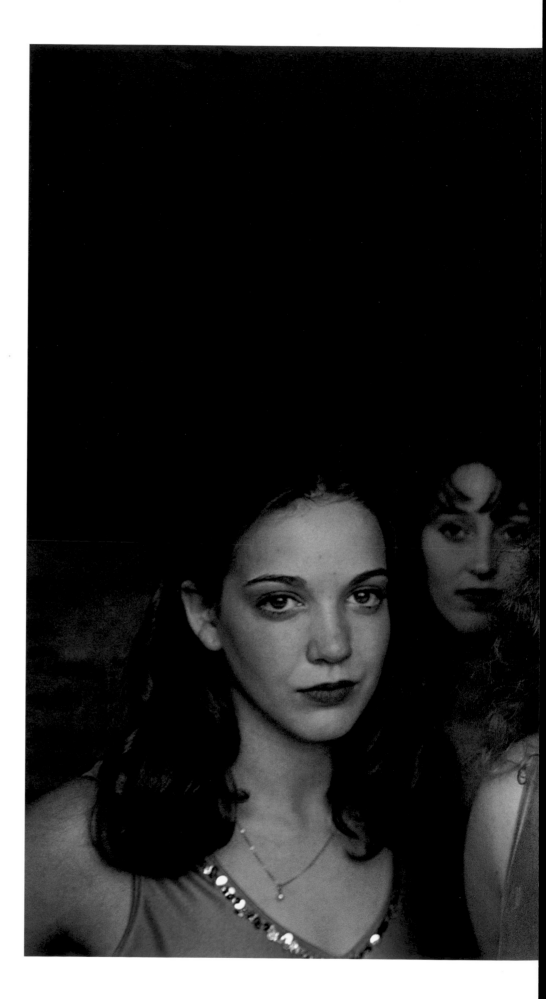

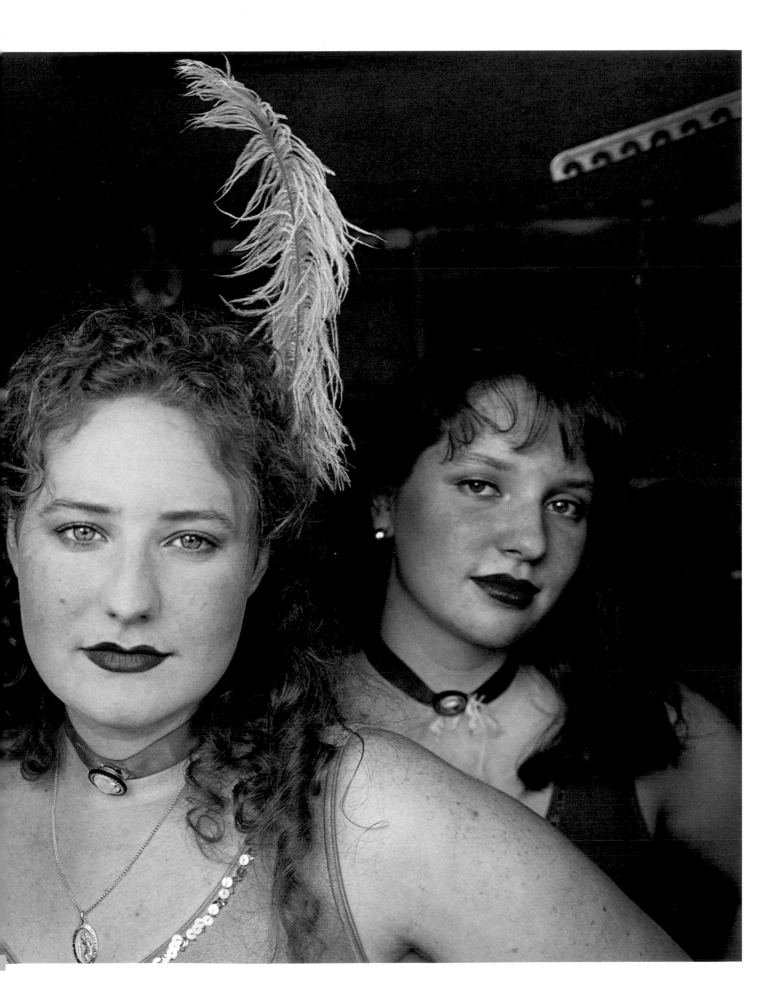

I think mud volleyball is interesting for a variety of reasons. First, you have women in bikinis rolling around in the mud. Second—I forget the other reasons.

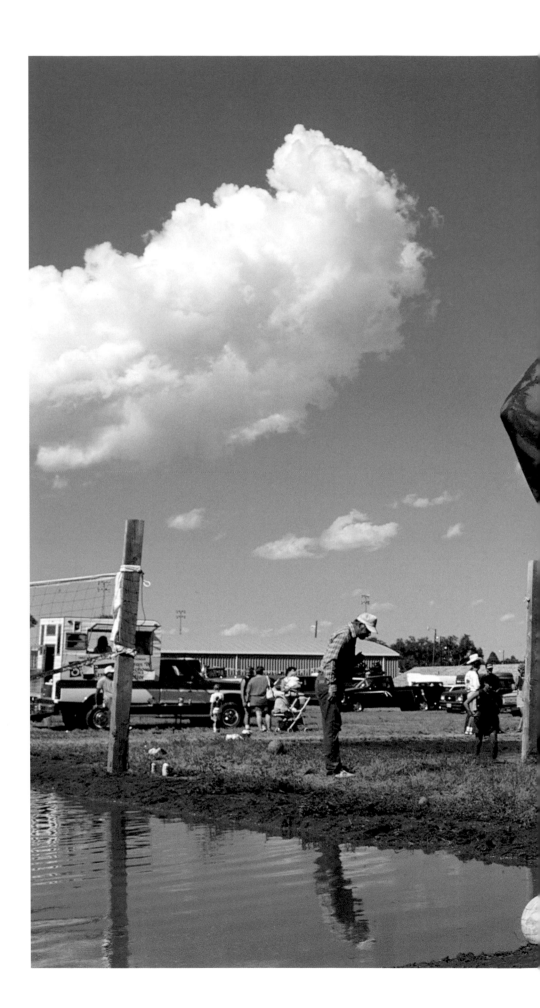

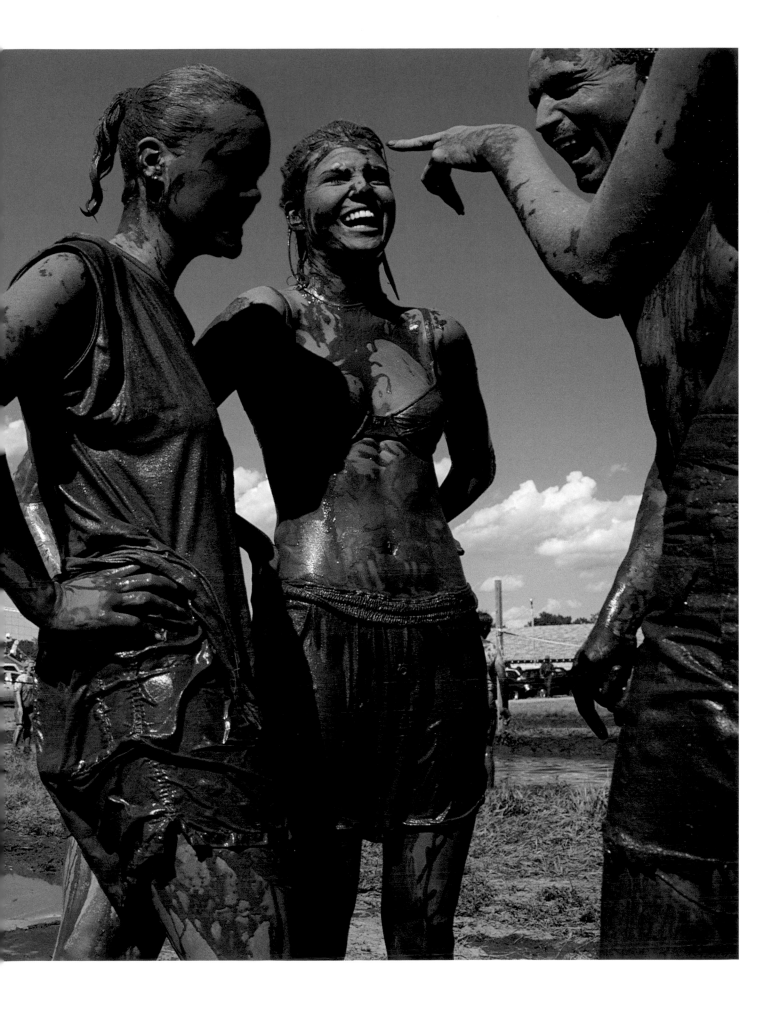

My favorite wacky thing about Nebraska is the Wayne Chicken Show. This town has had a long-standing poultry feud with nearby Wakefield, which actually produces millions of chickens and eggs every year. Wayne does not, but they have the festival anyway. Wakefield feels ripped off, and I can't say that I blame them. Shown here are the Chickendale Dancers, a group of "physically fit" men who put bags over their heads and strut their stuff in the fest's parade. Behind them is the official M.C. of the event, a guy in a chicken suit.

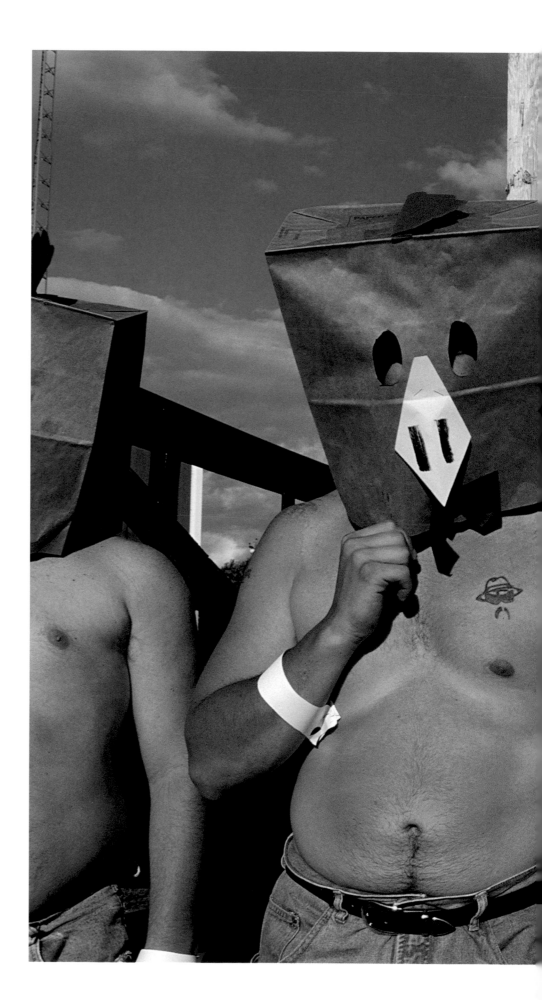

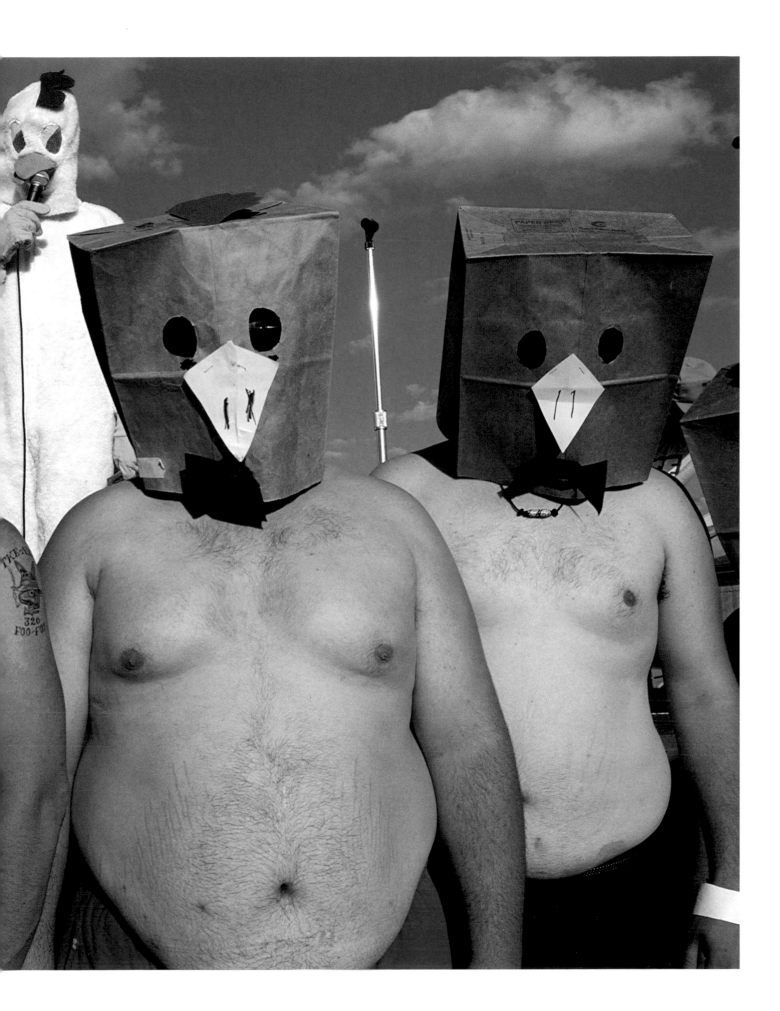

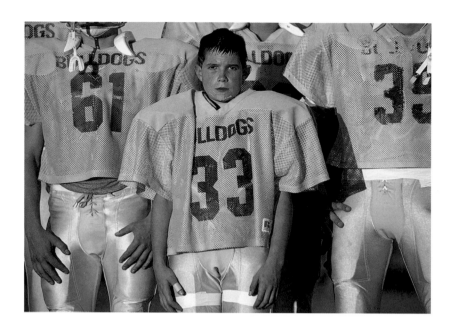

If your Nebraska school is so small that it can't field an eight-man football team, then the six-man version just may be the game for you. If you can walk, you can play, no matter how small you are. This was the Chester line-up that year. The consolidation of schools has meant that there are fewer six-man teams playing now, and that's a shame. These games are exciting. Get past the line of scrimmage and you're gone. Forty-point defeats are not uncommon. A sign along the highway still proudly proclaims Chester as the birthplace of six-man football. ▶ The Rising City team prays before a home game against Bradshaw. Bradshaw must have prayed harder—they won the game.

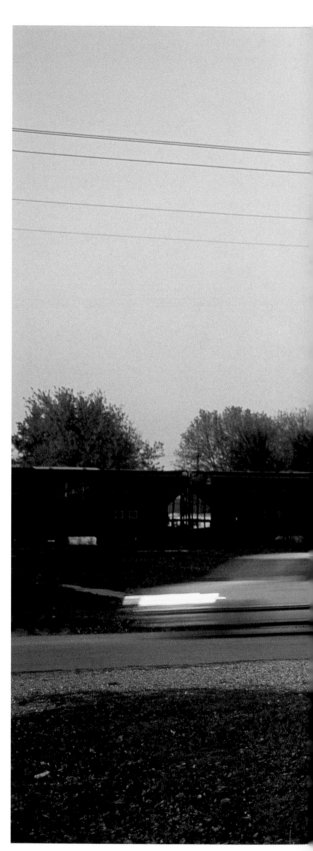

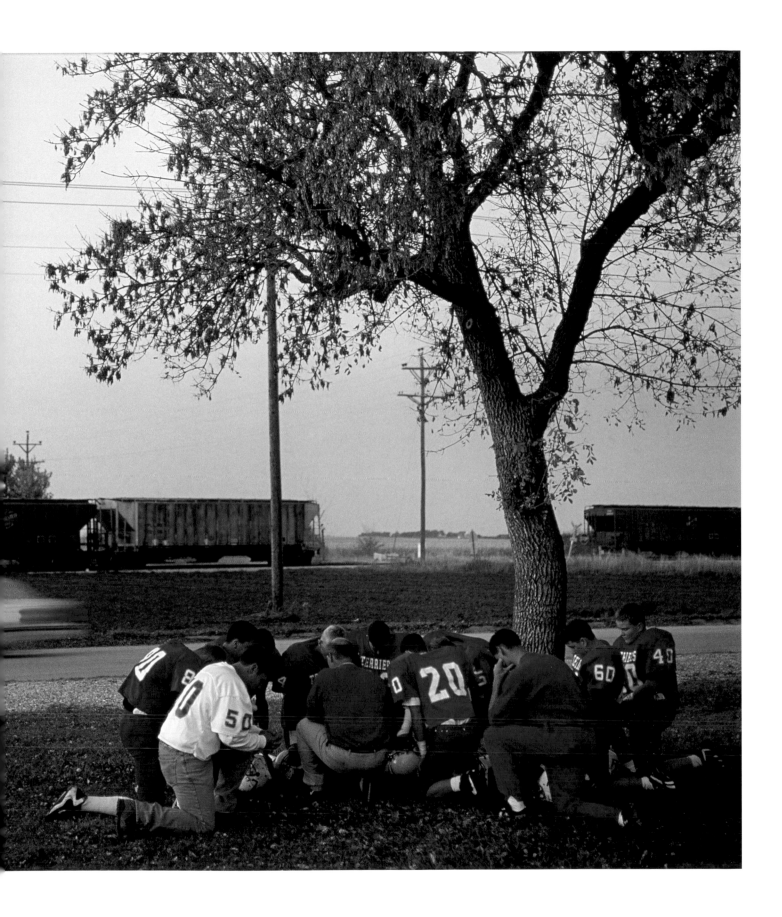

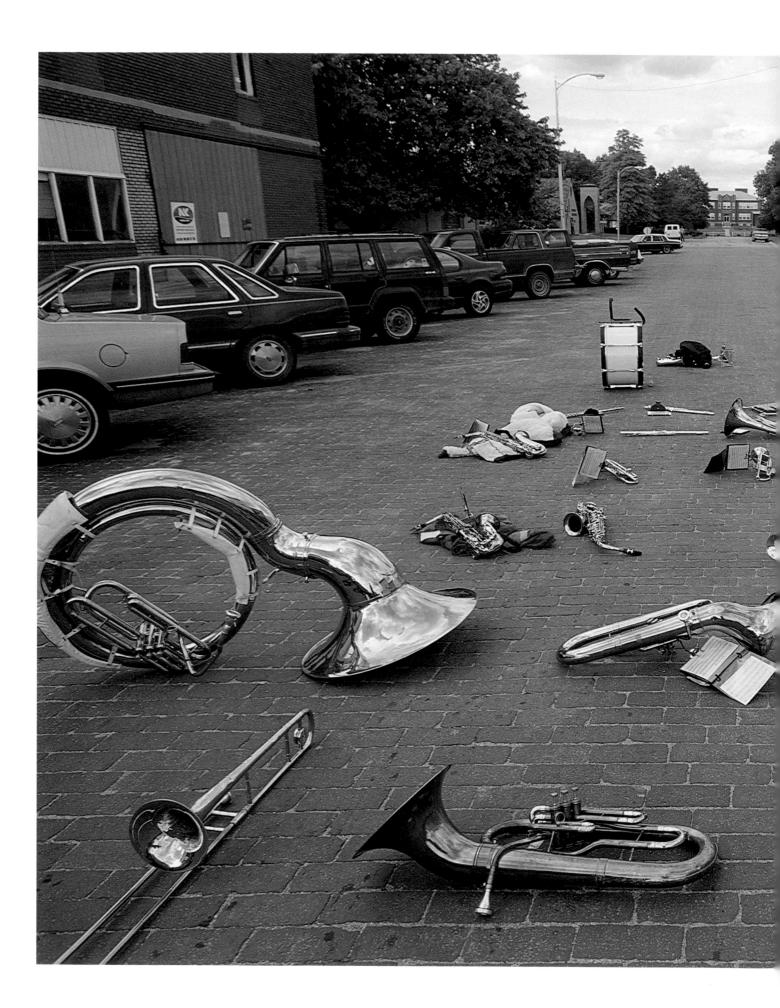

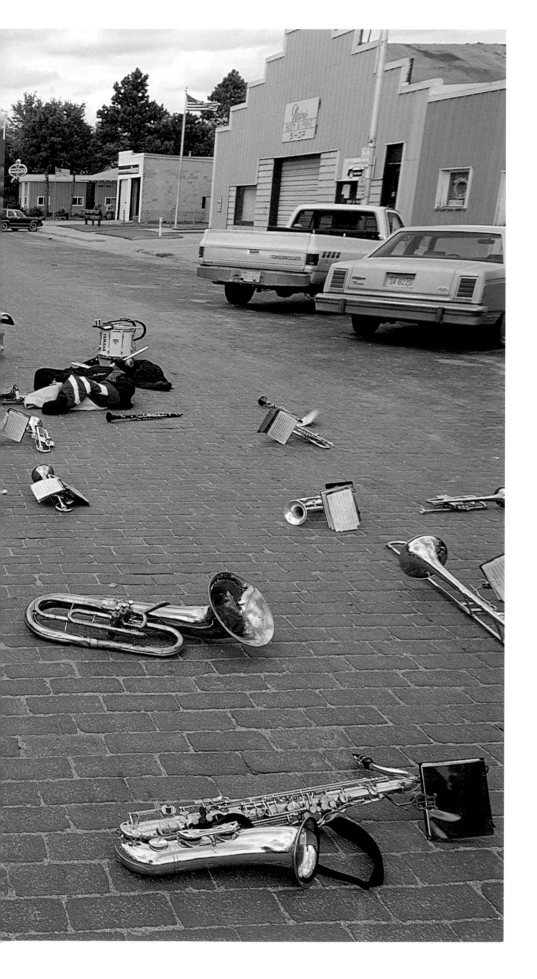

This tells you how small the town of Milligan is. After a parade one day the band members simply left their instruments on Main Street. And why worry? They knew nobody would be driving down the street because everyone in town was at the same pep rally they were headed to.

Fireworks finish off a small-town festival. The folks in the truck kept asking me if I wanted a beer. Bless their hearts.

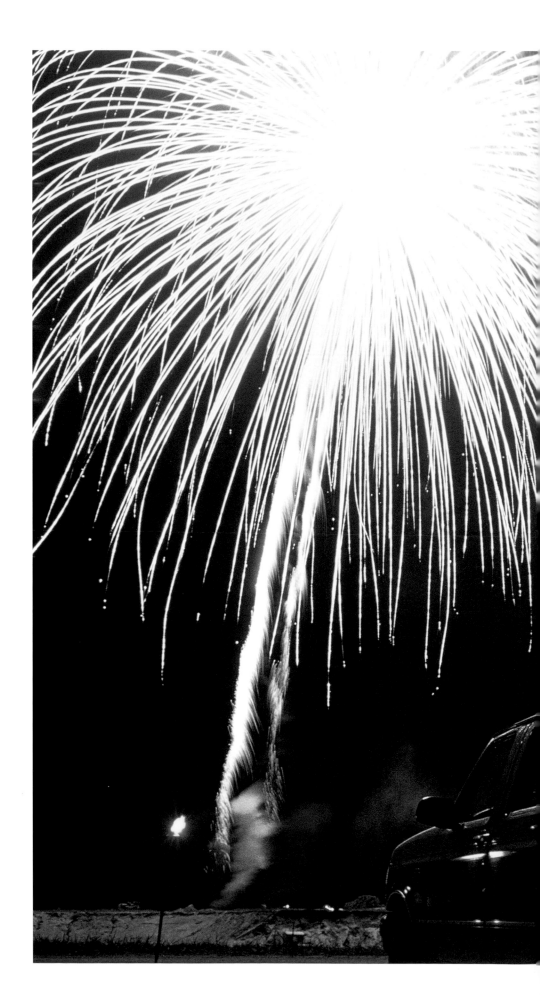

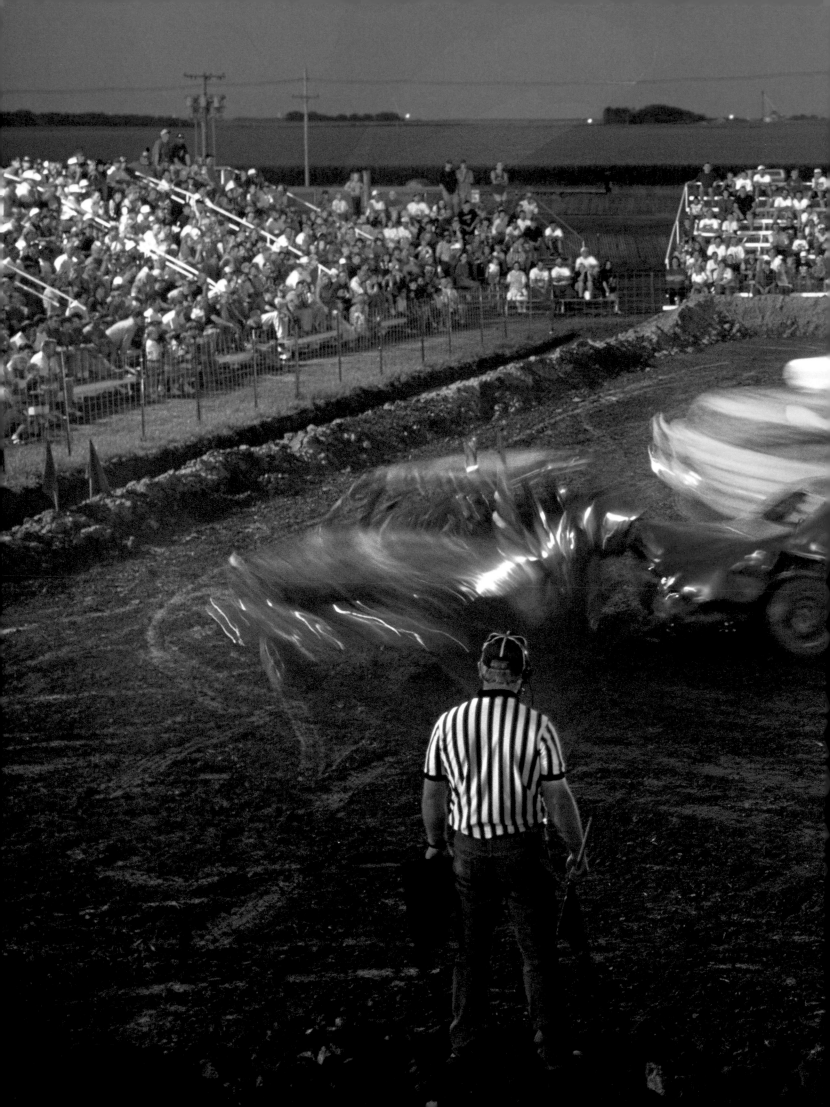

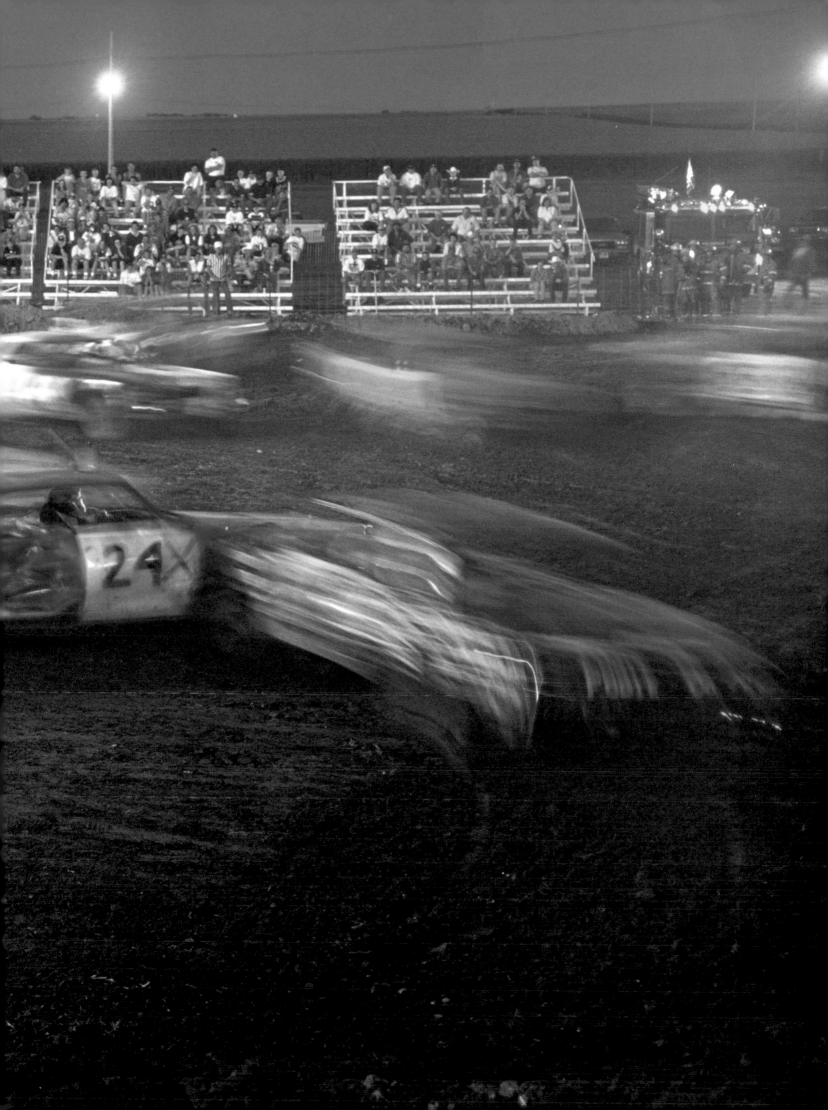

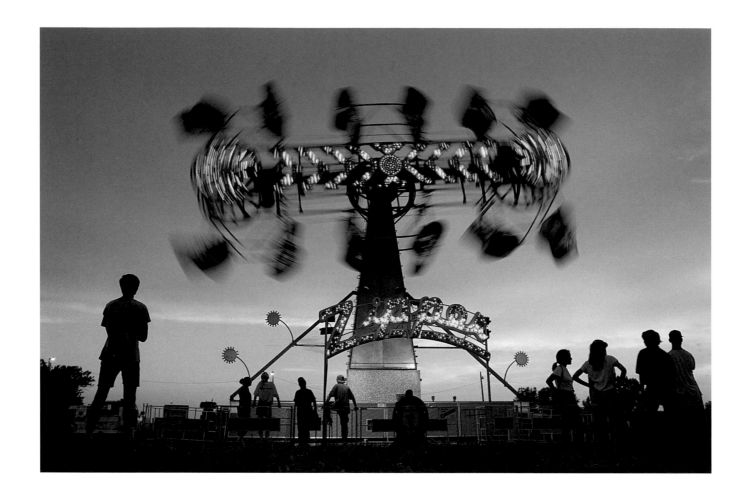

70   ◄ *(pages 68-69)* I think this is my favorite picture. Demolition derbies are fascinating. The goal is to keep your car running. They drive around in reverse because a car lasts longer smashing things up tail first. The last moving car wins. I came away all depressed from this evening, thinking I hadn't made a single usable frame out of a perfect situation—beautiful light, cornfields surrounding the place, small crowd. The problem with time exposure pictures is that you never know what you have until you see the film. I was all mopey driving the long two hours back to Lincoln, bummed out thinking I hadn't gotten a thing.

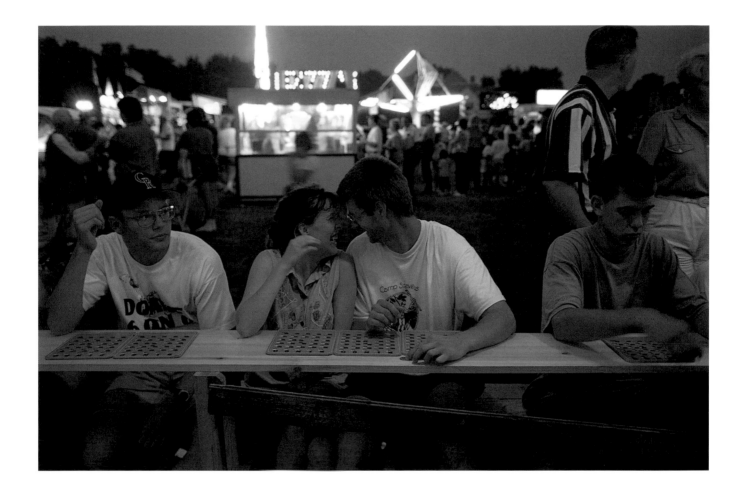

◄ Small towns are at their best when these little carnivals come through. This is the
high point of the summer. Stare at the Zipper long enough and you may start getting
queasy. ▲ This was in the town of Western. People were playing bingo with the carnival
going on behind them. They use a lot of yellow light bulbs out here to keep the bugs
from coming in. Since yellow light can make for better pictures, I stood in one place until
the bingo enthusiasts forgot about me. That's my goal when shooting. Just ignore me.

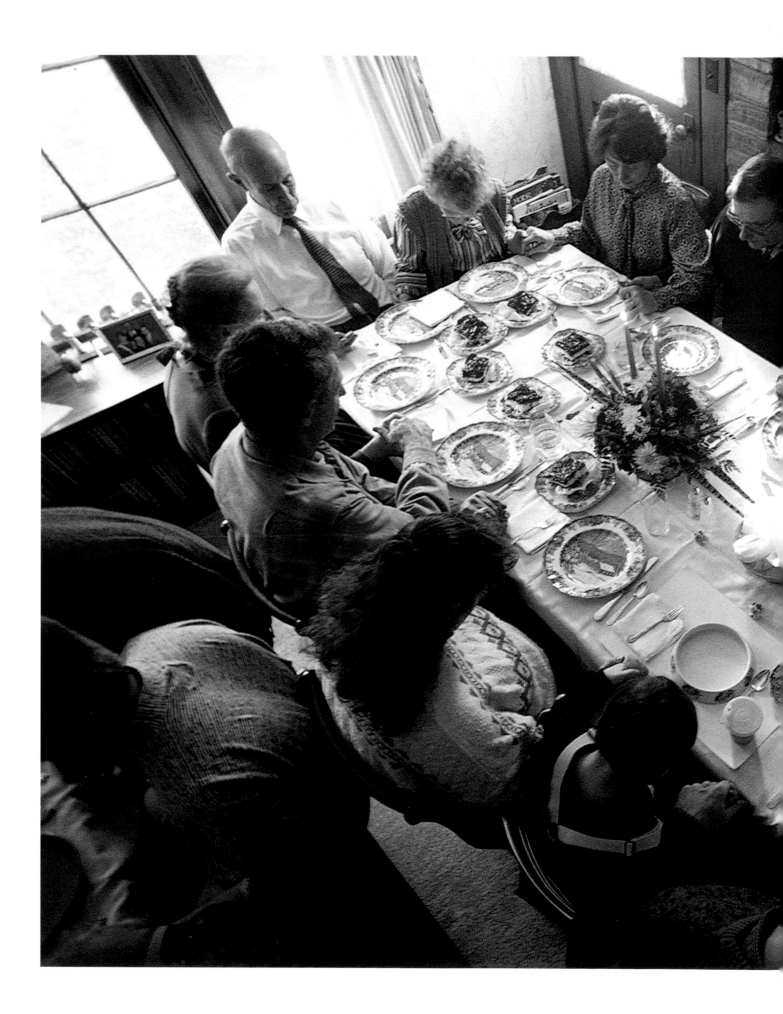

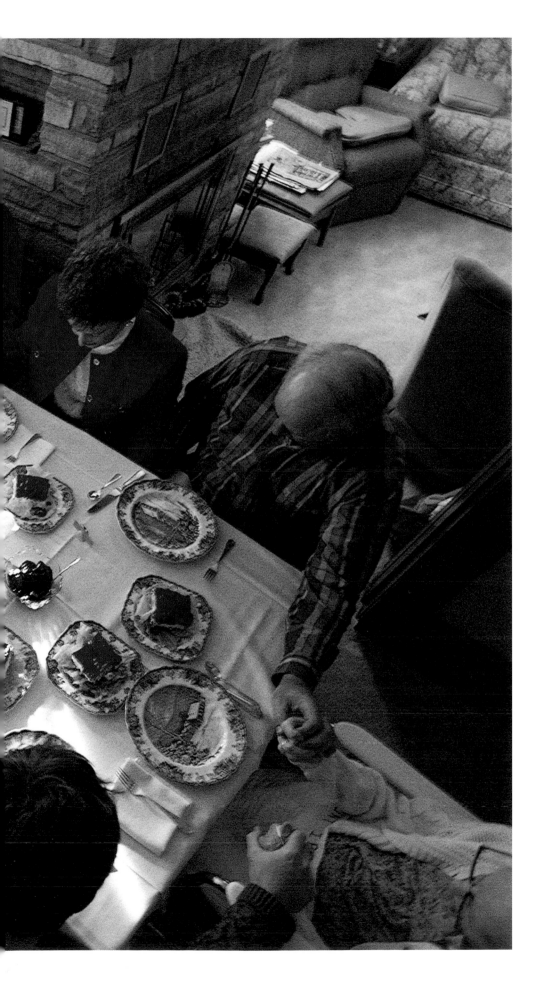

Nostalgia and a desire to imitate Norman Rockwell led me to this holiday dinner at the Trumble farmstead near Papillion. Note the pheasant tail feathers in the centerpiece. Many families say grace here still, including my own, but I confess we sometimes forget when we're really hungry.

Something I love about photography is that it opens doors. I had called this farm family for the first time just a few days before and invited myself to their house for Thanksgiving dinner. They said, "Sure! Come on over!" After an enormous meal I found myself standing on a chair in the middle of their living room. The adults were so full of food that they lay strewn about, unable or unwilling to move. The kids liked this and proceeded to bounce from lump to lump.

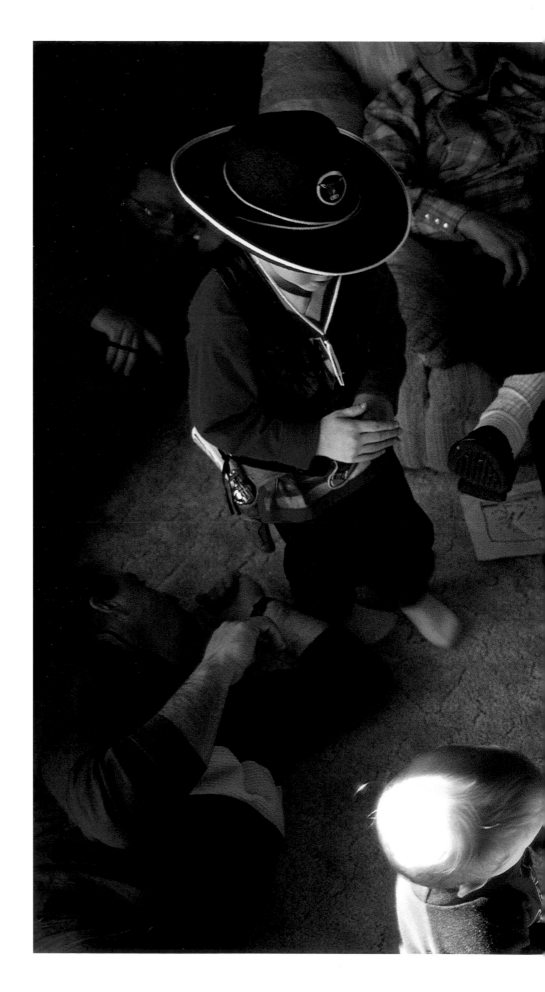

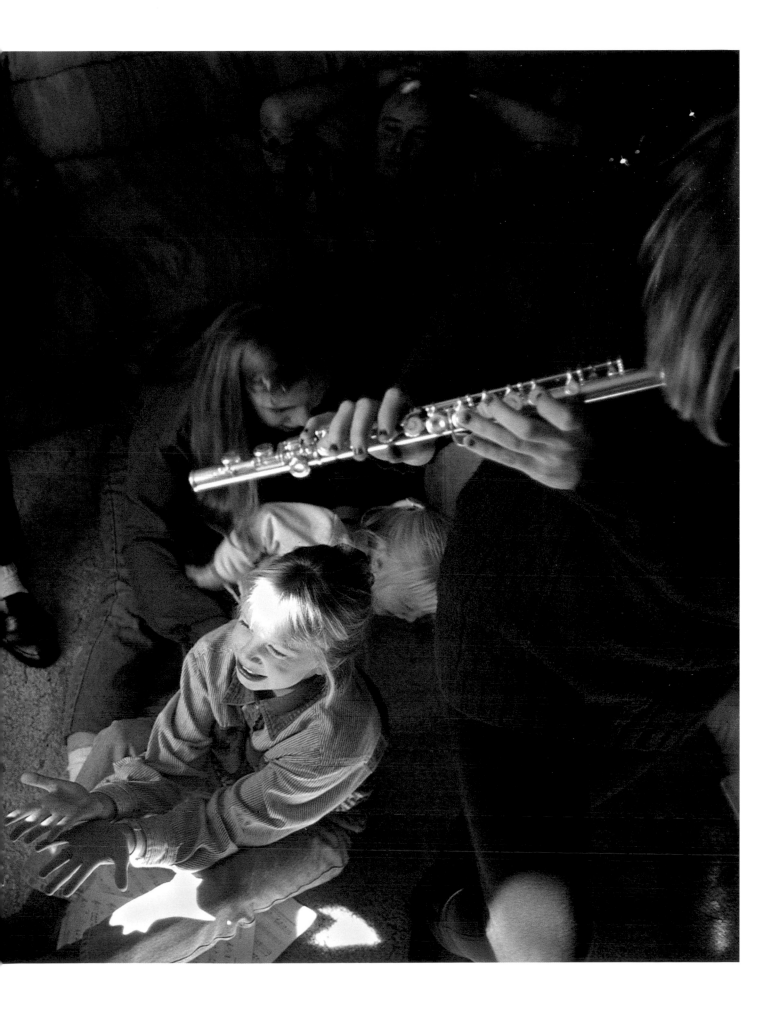

This was at the Buschkoetter family farm in south central Nebraska. This family was the subject of a documentary film called *The Farmer's Wife*. The film hadn't come out yet, but we all knew they were about to become famous. The girls didn't care though. Everyone in the family had been filmed so much that it was like I wasn't even there—perfect.

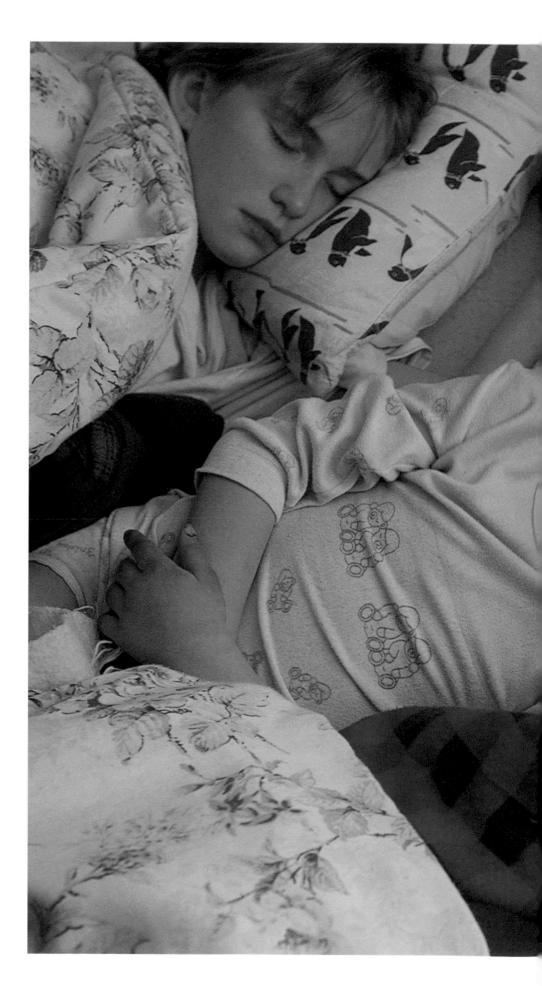

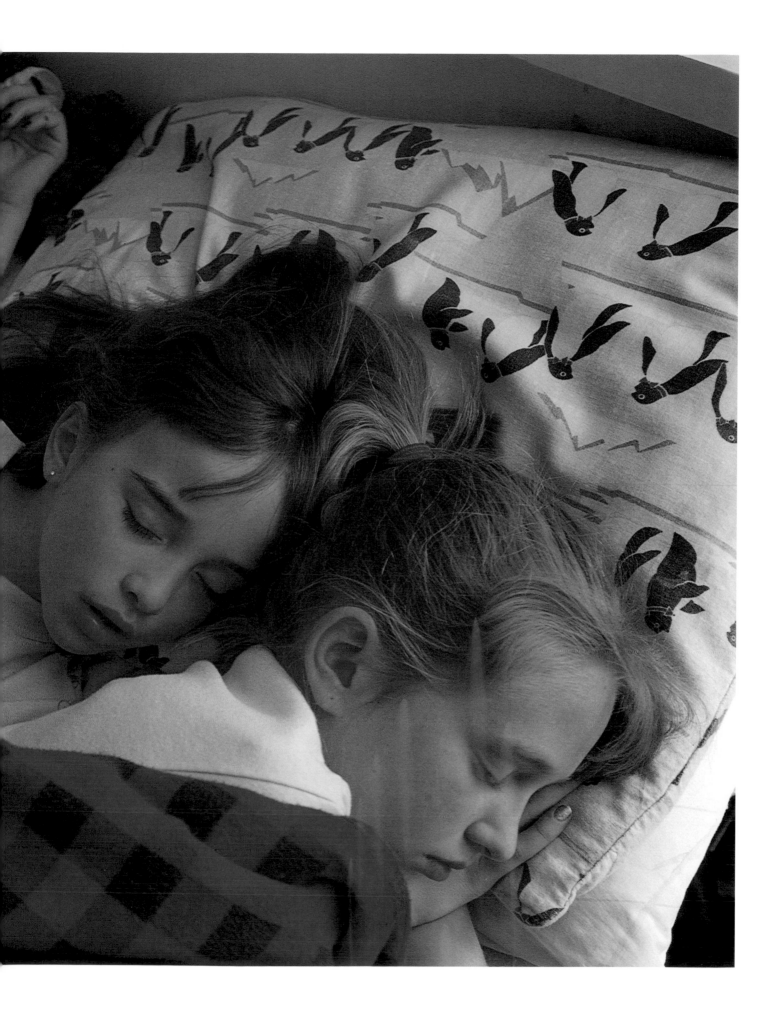

We study wildlife. We hunt it.

Sometimes we simply want

to view it from afar. Mainly

we just want to know it's out

there. Nebraskans have to know.

It's in our nature.

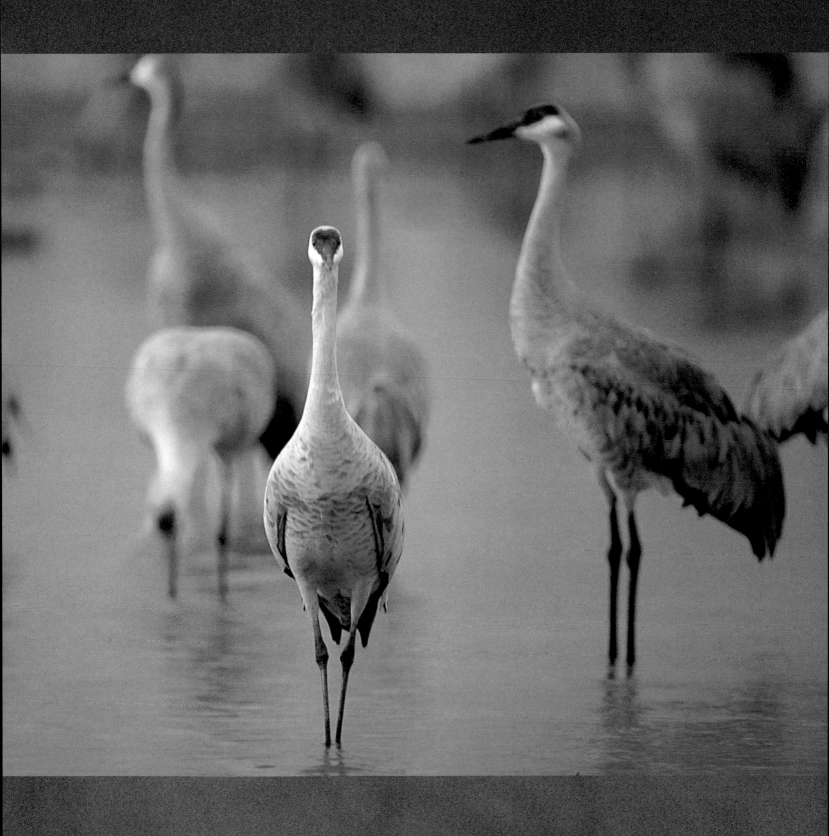

SANDHILL CRANES ON THE ROOST, PLATTE RIVER NEAR GIBBON

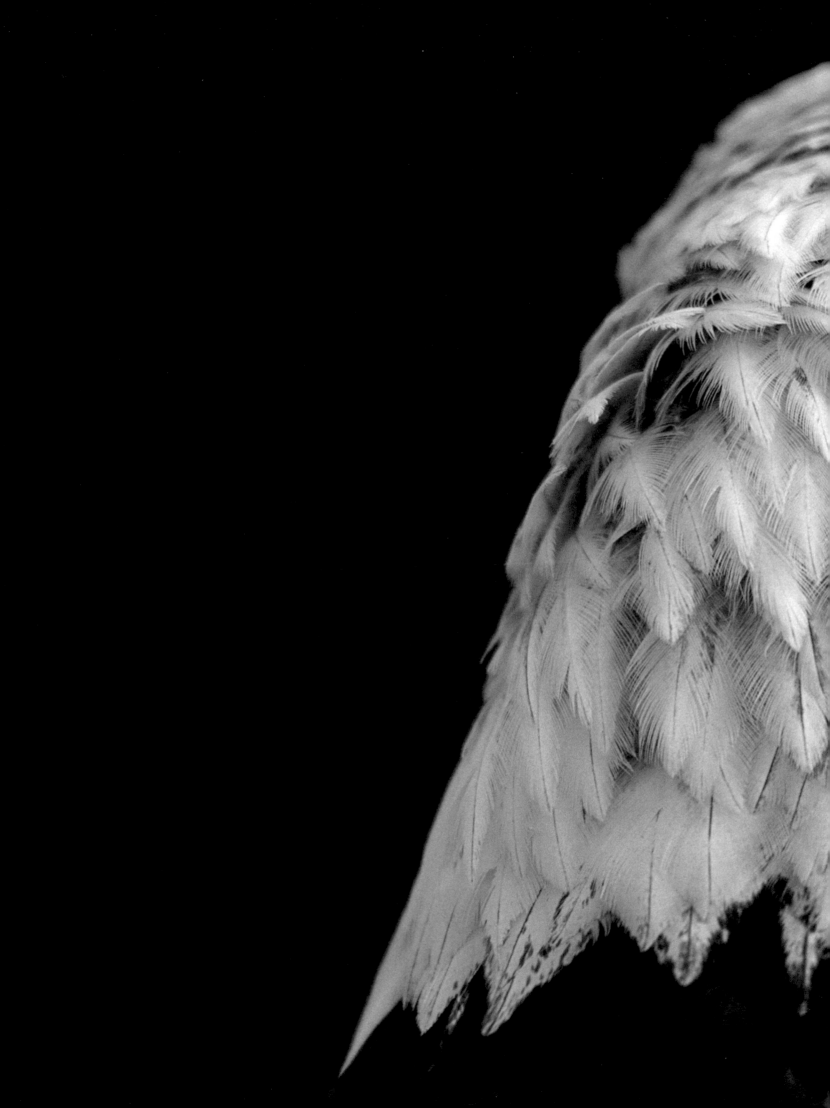

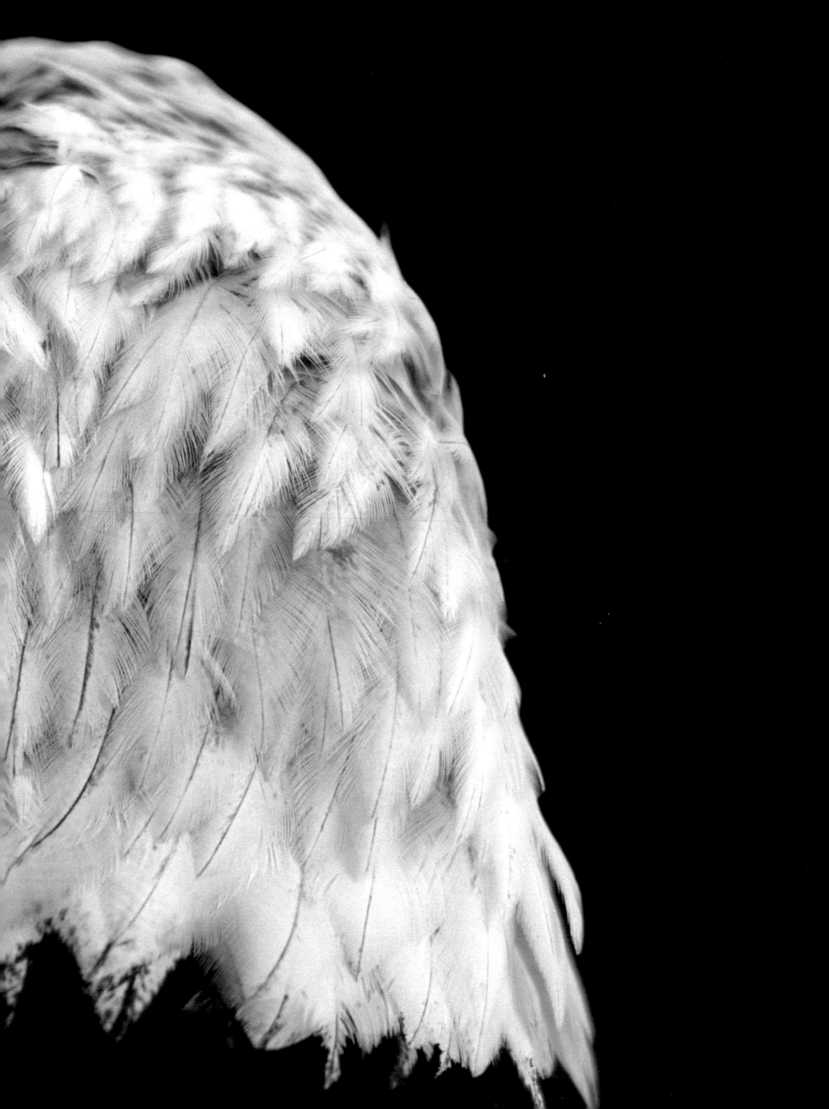

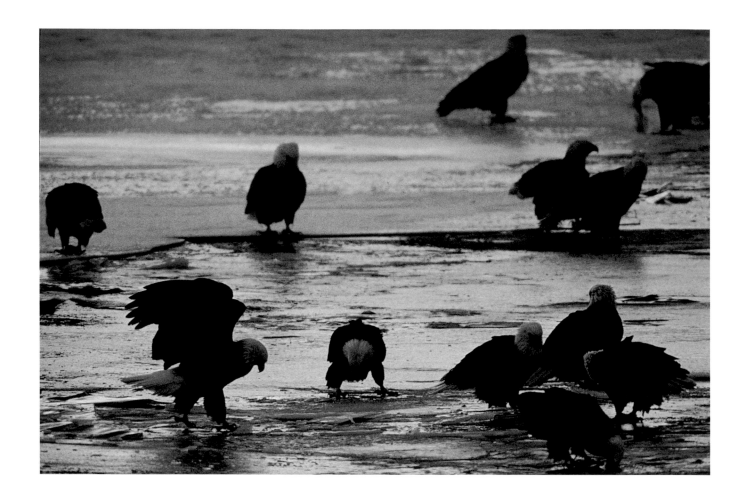

Bald eagles, thick as can be, gather on a mostly frozen Lake Ogallala. They're looking for fish that have been stunned as they pass through the hydro turbines at a dam. The colder the weather, the more birds they have. A guy named Rodger Knaggs runs the hydro dam out there. He calls me every once in a while and says, "We've got your bald eagles right here Joel. We've got 200 eagles right here. You head out and we'll get you some eagle pictures." Of course, the lake is a six-hour drive from me, and by the time I get there the eagles are sometimes gone, but what the hell. ▶ Sometimes you don't have to look very far for wildlife. After having goldfinches repeatedly fly into the windows at my farm, I figured I'd better put up a feeder to distract them. In the spring, when they're in full breeding plumage, it's like having your own flock of pet canaries.

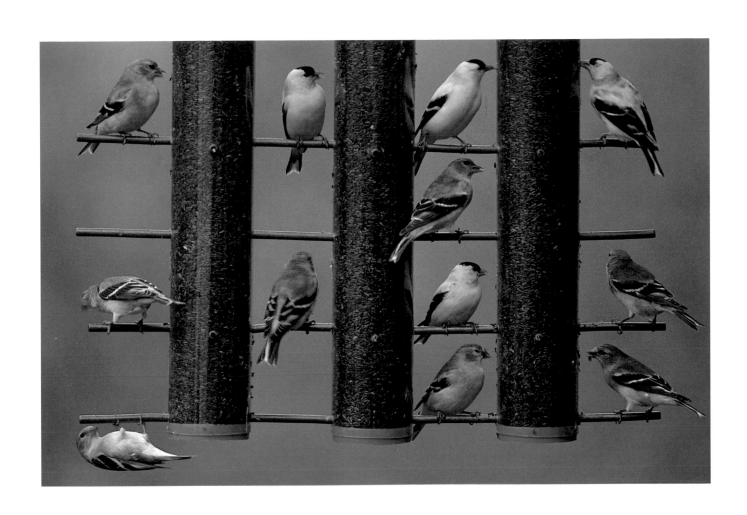

The evening flight of sandhill cranes to their Platte River roost is one of the great wildlife spectacles on this continent. After sunset, the darker it gets, the better it gets. Imagine thousands of gray ghosts calling out in air so dark blue you can barely see them. The sounds alone make this a great life experience.

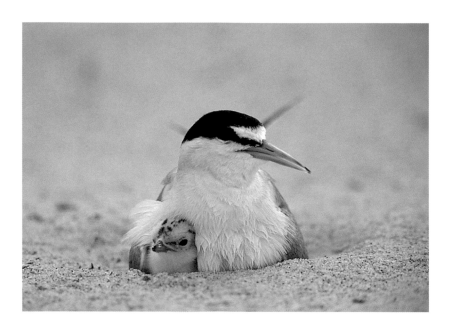

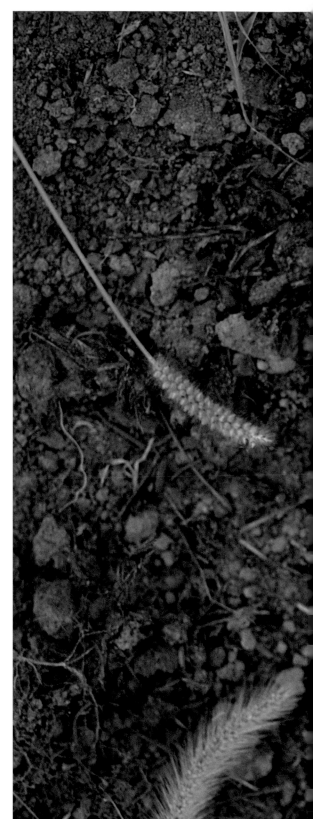

Rodger the eagle guy also got me close to some least terns for a few minutes. There is a section of beach that the terns nest in. They dive bomb anyone who comes around, repeatedly striking from above (Rodger stayed in his truck). I hurried and took my picture before an incoming bird punctured my head.

▶ This is the American burying beetle. This endangered insect was photographed near Gibbon. The biologist I met there had captured it to study and was getting ready to let it go. He said the beetle would bury the dead mourning dove overnight. If it finds a mate, it lays its eggs in an underground chamber near the body, then uses the dove as a "beetle grocery store," providing food for its young. That's some pretty good social behavior for a bug.

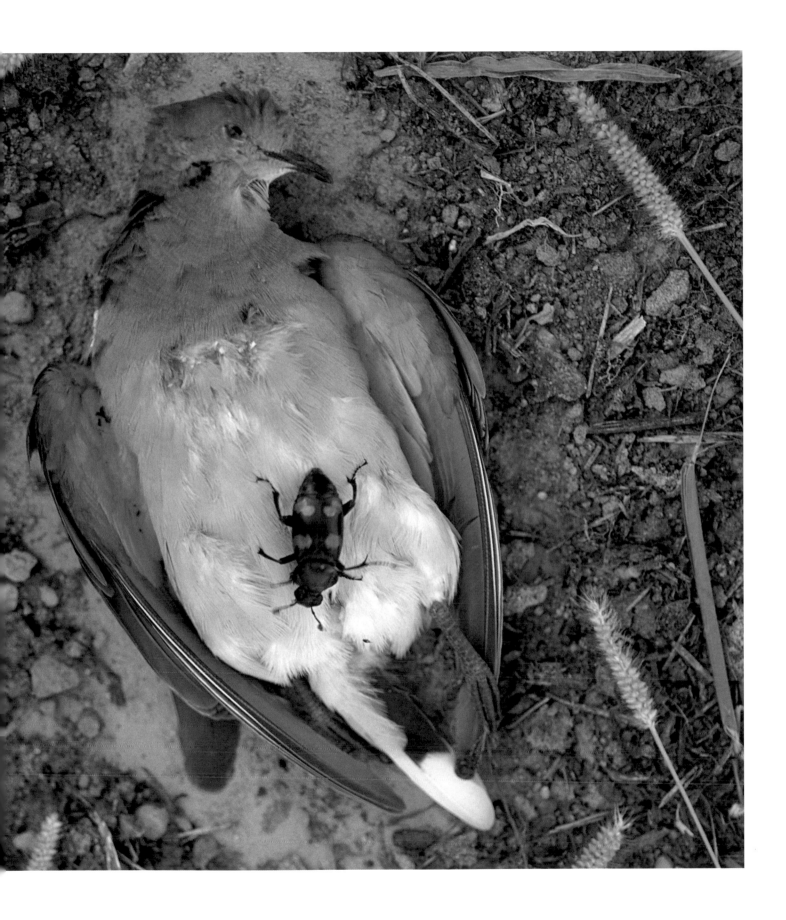

Abundant wide-open spaces mean we have wildlife. This is near Valentine at the Fort Niobrara National Wildlife Refuge. The buffalo in front has a raised tail. This indicates that I've frightened him and he's going to take a poop. That bit of trivia doesn't really add to the drama or beauty of the scene much, but I thought you would want to know.

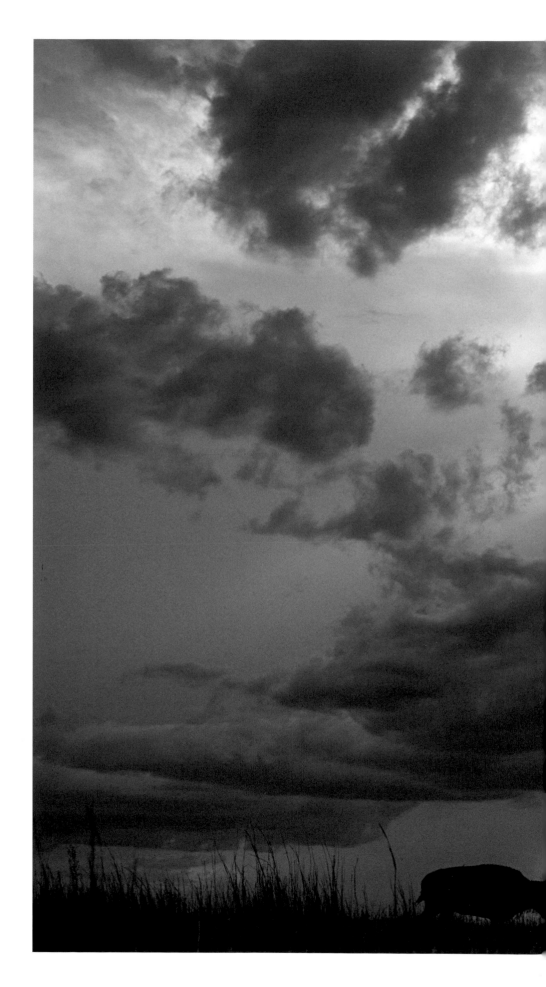

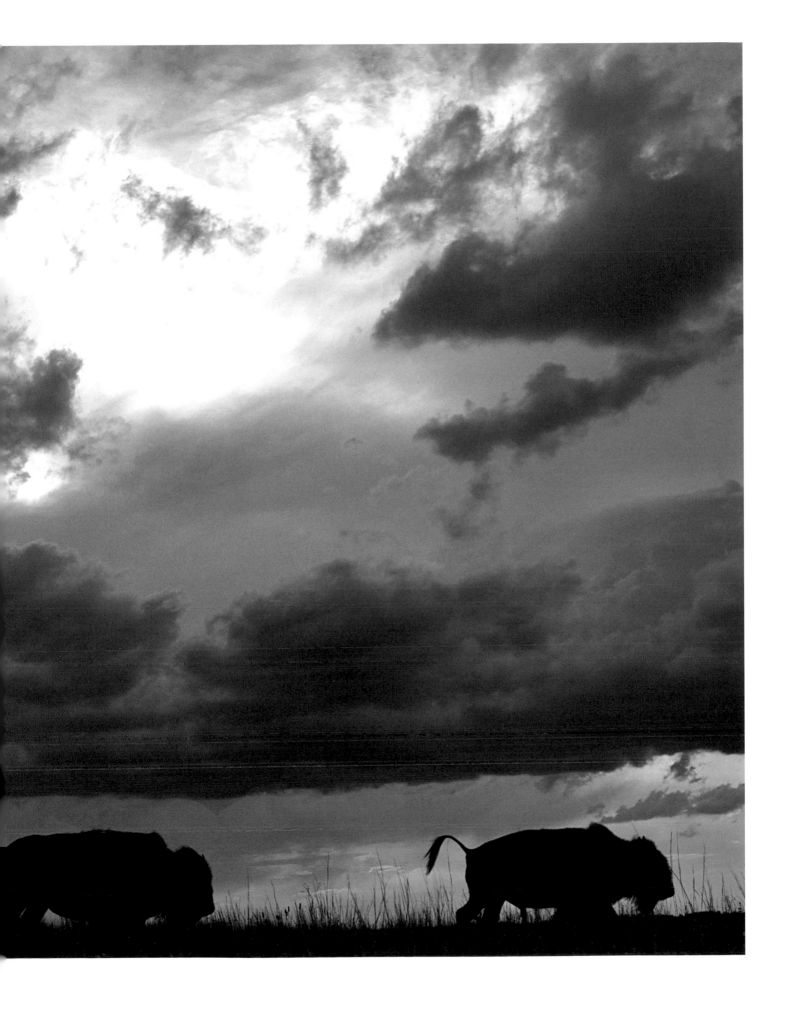

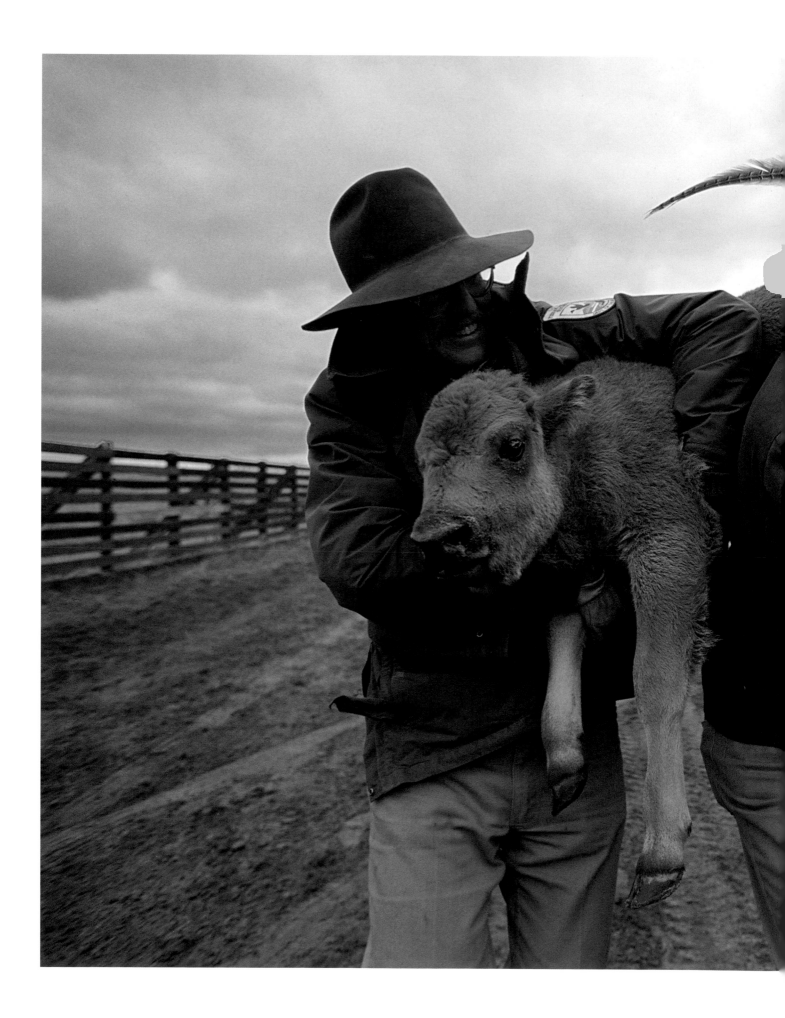

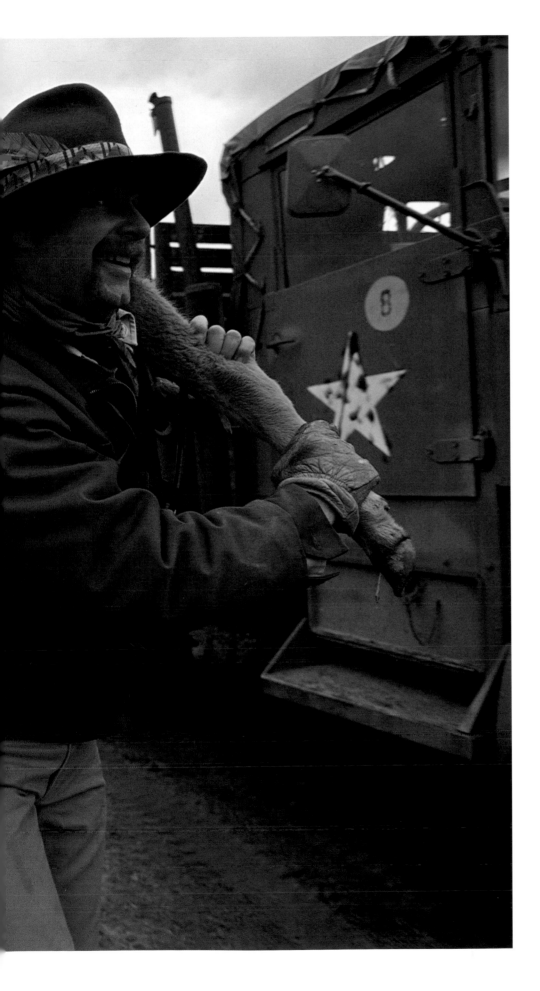

The annual bison roundup at Fort Niobrara's refuge is a hoot, mainly because bison don't like to be rounded up. Fences are just a bluff to them, and refuge workers get to experience the occasional stampede when trying to gather the herd. This calf was being carried back to a pen containing his mother. Refuge manager Royce Huber summed it up this way: "You pretty much herd them any way they want to go."

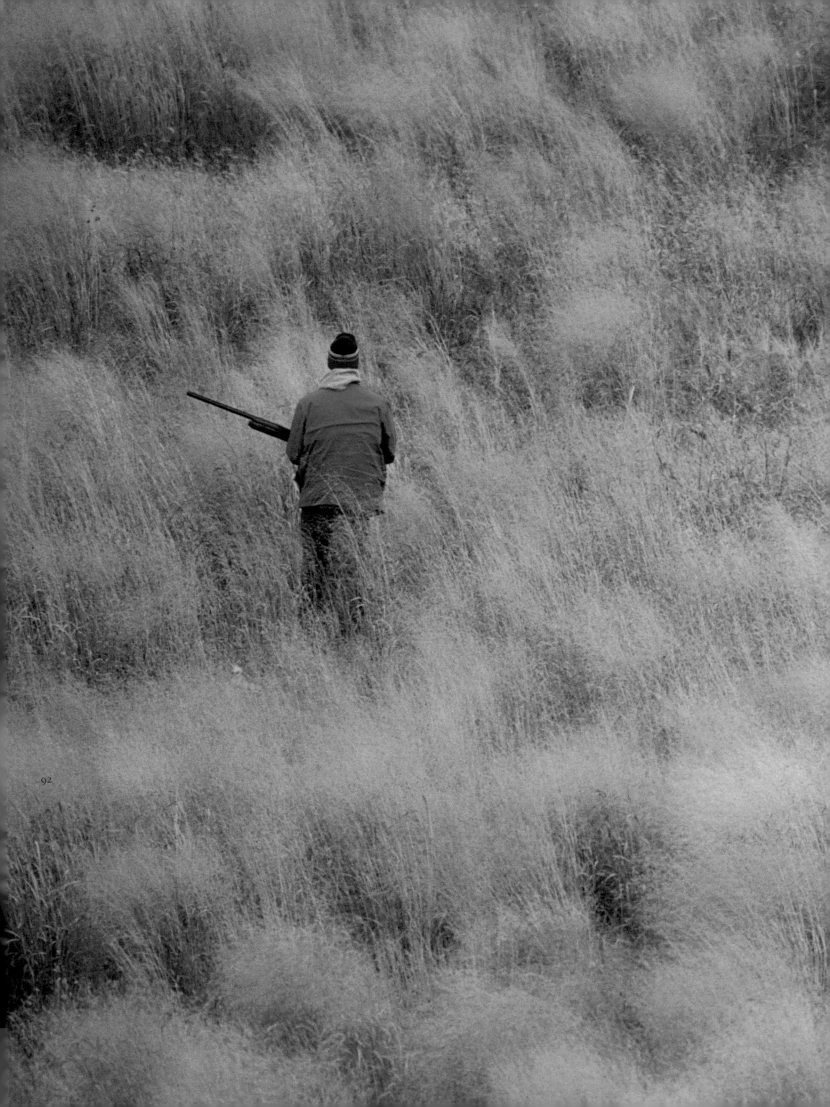

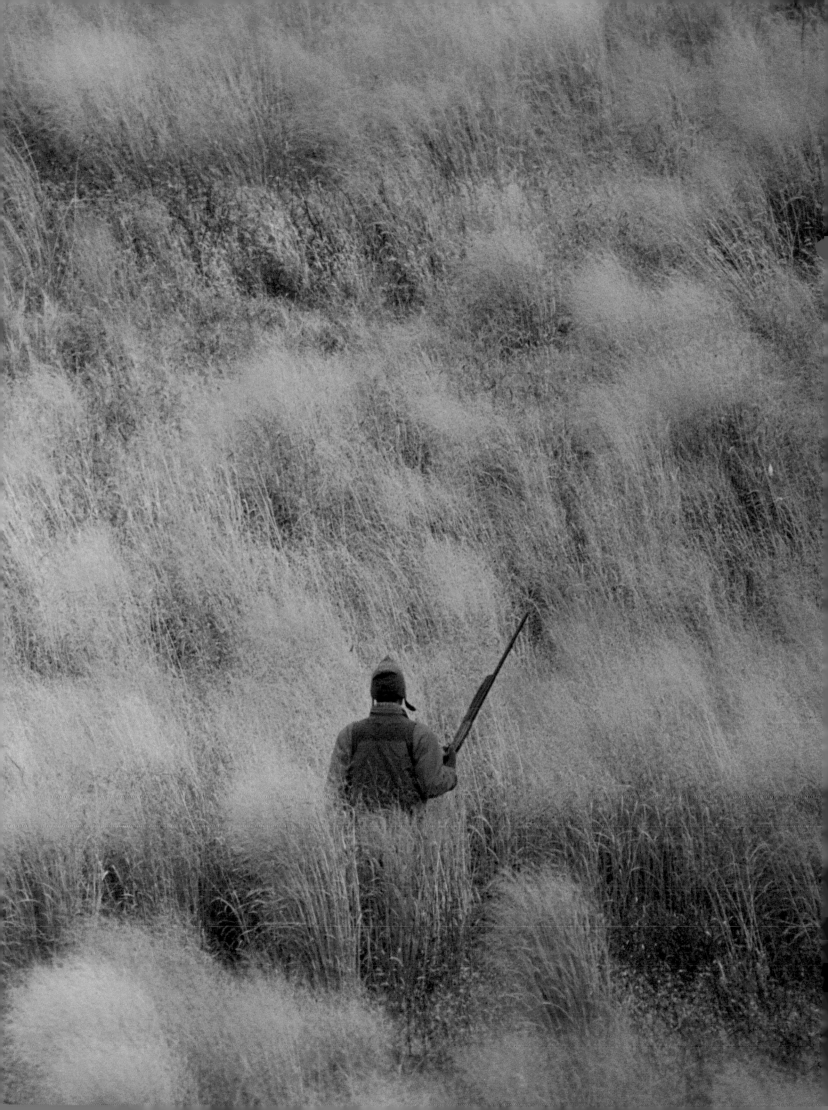

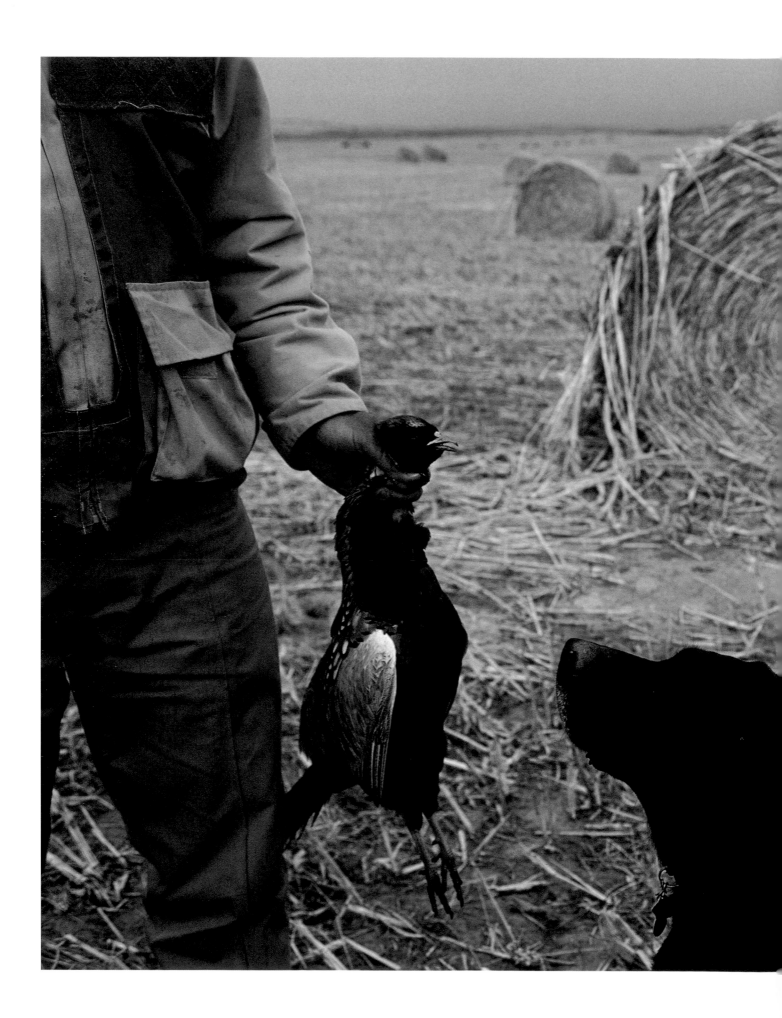

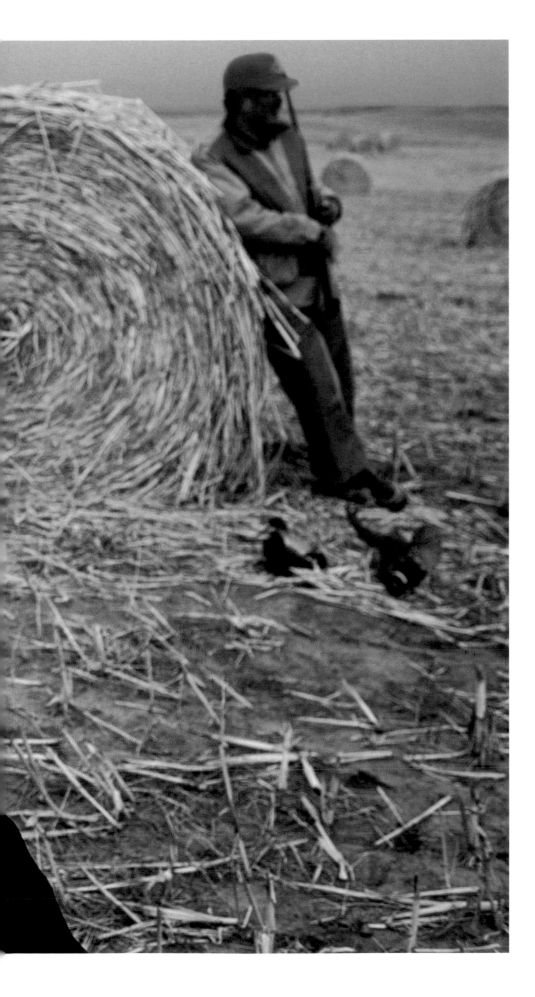

▲ *(pages 92-93)* I've gone out hunting with my father and brother for years. We didn't care if we shot any birds or not; the highlight of the day was lunch. In fact, sometimes we'd often find ourselves questioning why we were hunting in the first place. Clearly it was simply the chance to be together. I think many people hunt for the same reason. On this day I carried a camera instead of a gun. I'd hunted this field all my life but was always nervous, worrying about whether a pheasant would explode at my feet or not. That day was different. I concentrated on the texture and color of the grass. Showing the palette of color in that grassy hillside made the whole day worthwhile for me.

◄ This is at Broken Bow during their "One Box Pheasant Hunt," when everyone rolls out the red carpet once a year for hundreds of visiting hunters. This is a hunting contest in which teams of four hunters split one box of shells and see how many pheasants they can get. There are 24 shells in a box, so each guy gets 6 shells. It's really hard to get your limit with just six shots, because pheasants, when they flush, don't stick around to say good-bye.

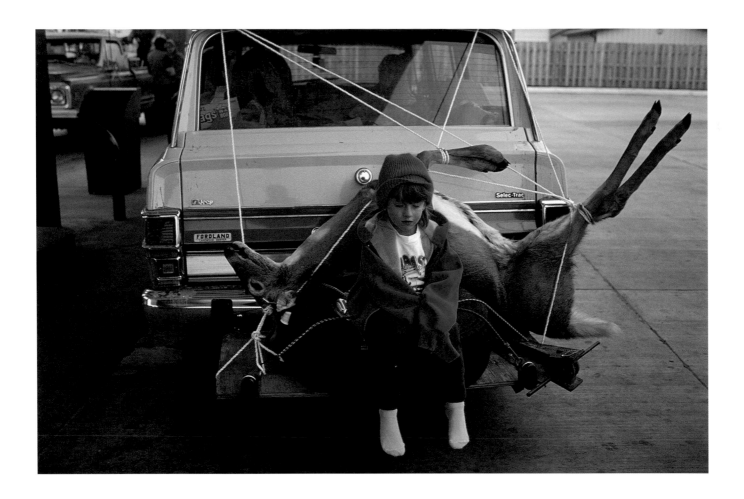

Leaving Broken Bow, I was just stopping to get gas on the way out of town and saw this scene. Notice how everyone's wearing orange? That's so they don't shoot each other. There are no orange deer. If you go out wearing an antler hat, you're going to get blasted.

▶ This was shot in southeast Nebraska near the Missouri River. There was a notice on a cafe bulletin board that said the members of the Nebraska Catfishing Club were about to gather. Sounds too good to be true, eh? I drove all over the county looking for catfishermen, but there had been flooding and hardly anyone was fishing. Toward the end of the day I finally came upon a couple of guys that had been drinking and fishing, in that order. They wanted to know where I got all of that fancy camera gear.

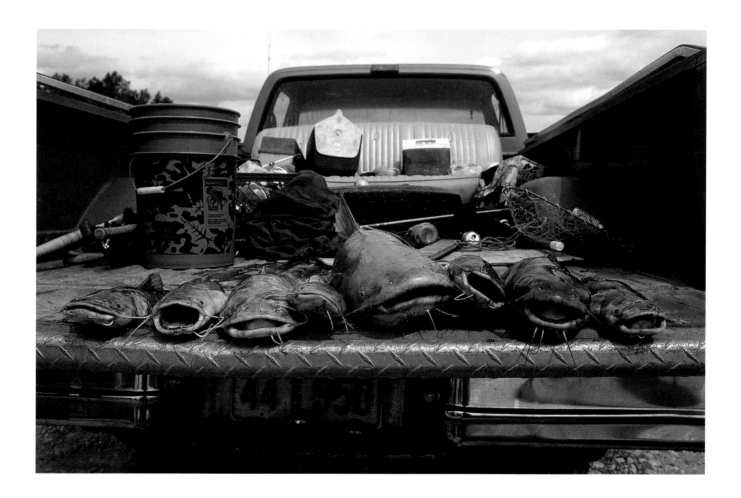

► *(pages 98-99)* Cabela's, the "World's Largest Outfitter," has a man-made mountain in the back of their huge store where stuffed animals strike life-like poses on fake rocks. Any time I see anything that's stuffed, the photographer in me thinks, "Hey, they have to clean that thing once in awhile." So I called up and asked, "When do you dust the sheep?" You have to ask some pretty odd questions in my business.

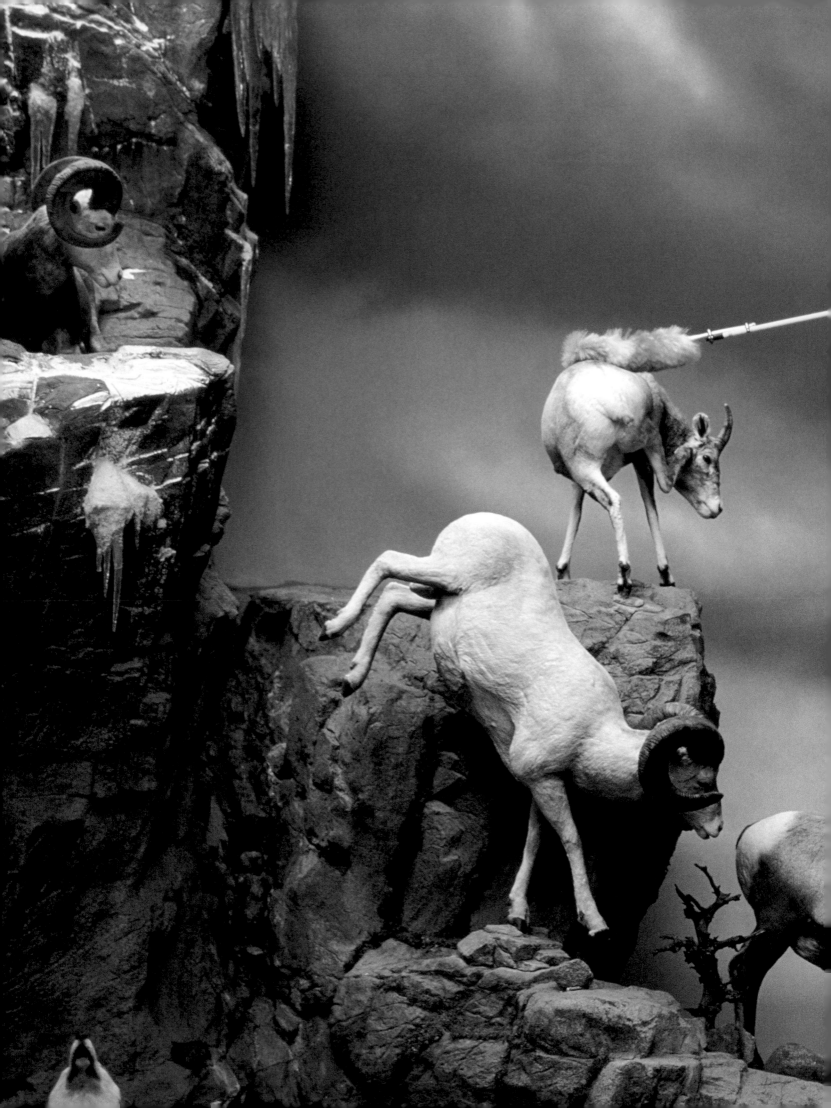

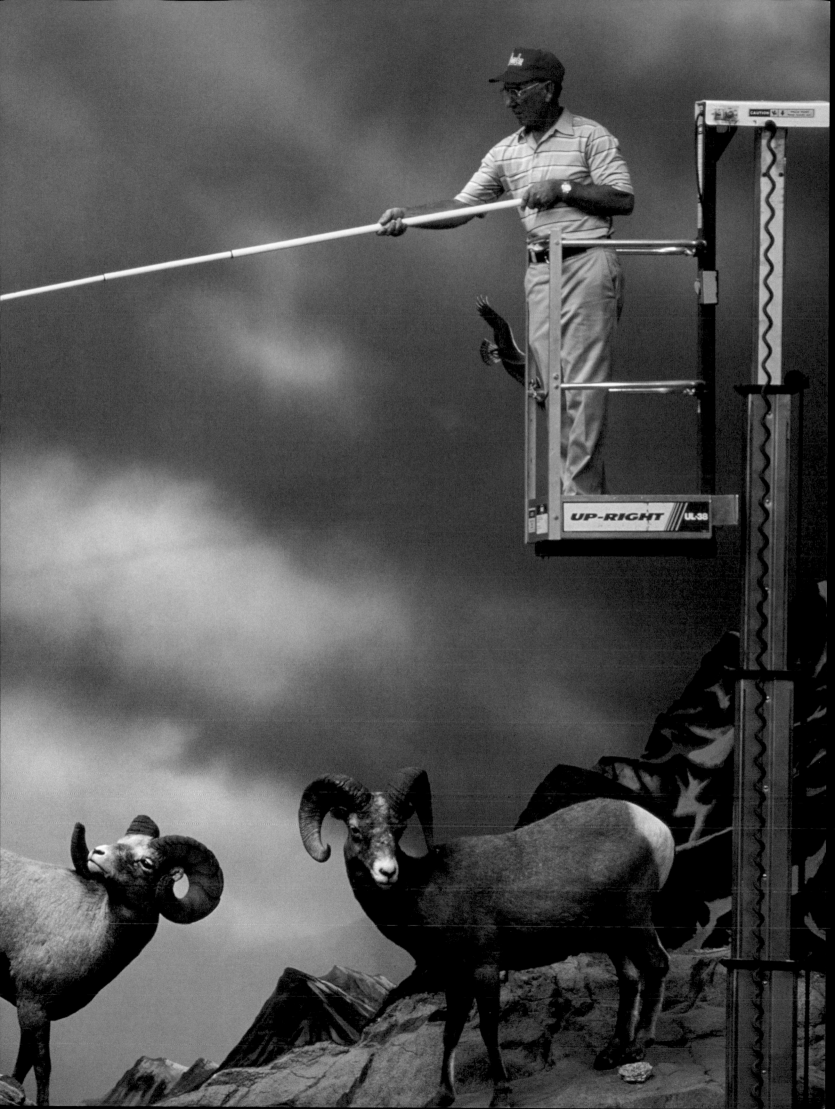

In Nebraska, most of the time

it's too wet. Or too dry.

Or too hot. Or too cold.

But not all the time.

And that's what keeps us going.

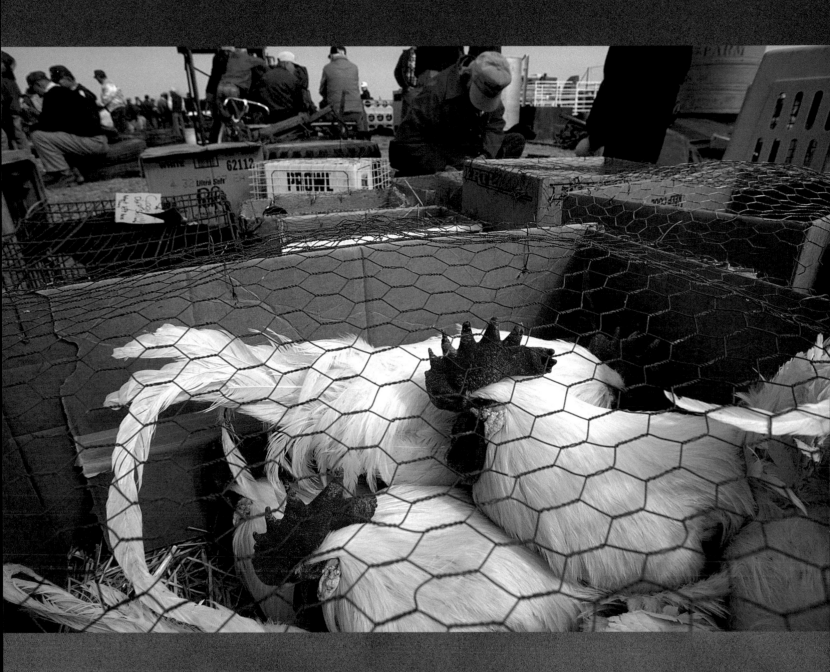

CHICKENS TO GO, COMMUNITY AUCTION, FRIEND

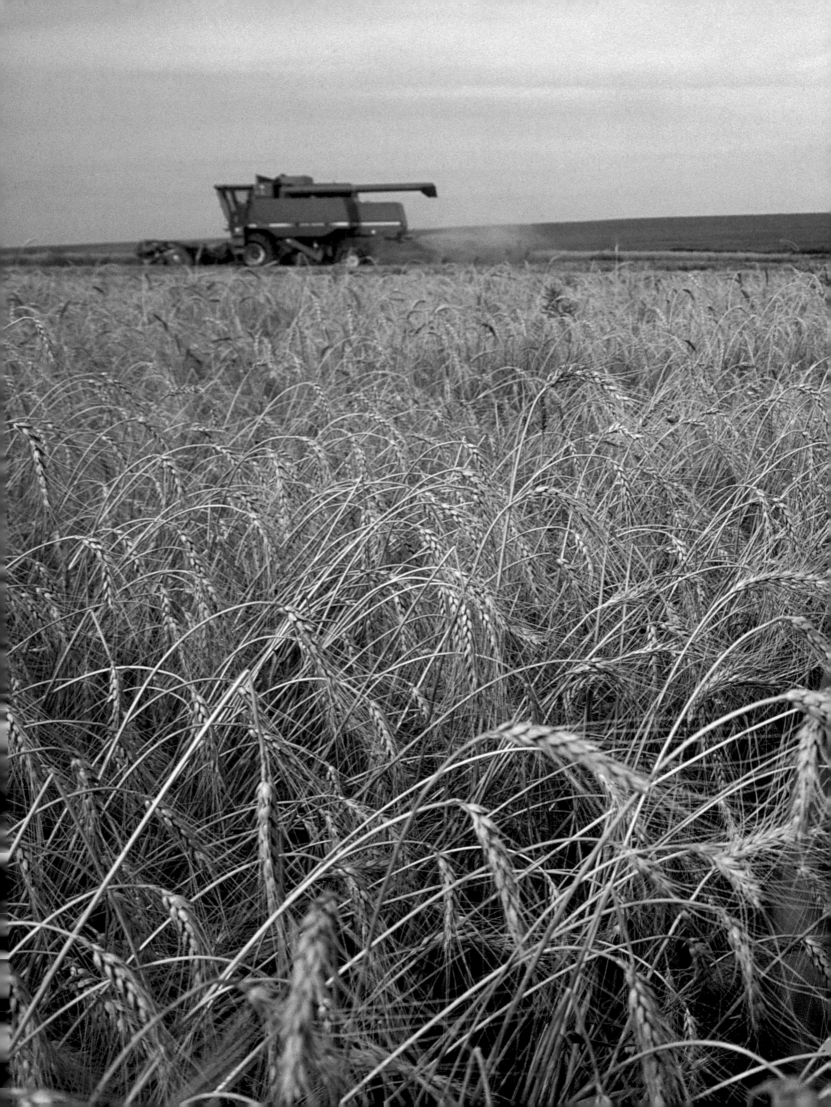

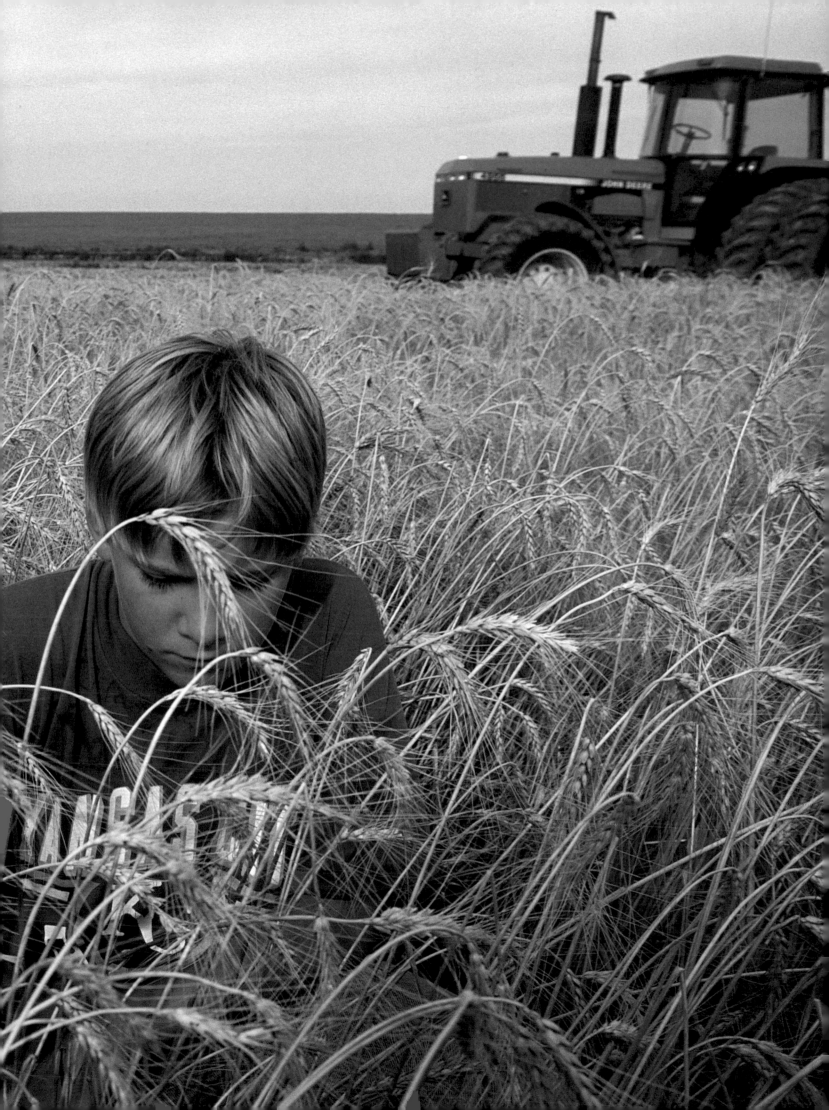

◀ *(pages 102-103)* This boy was not old enough to drive the combine, but he was old enough to drive the tractor. Driving the tractor means you get bored sometimes. The combine is where all the action is. So we were just passing time out in the wheat field, waiting for the combine to dump his grain into the grain cart behind the tractor. It's subtle stuff, but Nebraska is like that at times. That's very comforting to me, and I want it to stay that way. I like the fact that it seems like 1958 here.

▶ Farm guys tend to wear a jacket until there is literally nothing left of it. I asked this guy why he didn't get a new jacket, and all he could say was, "What for?" Rotten clothing adds atmosphere to any photo, and let me say for the record, I'm all for it.

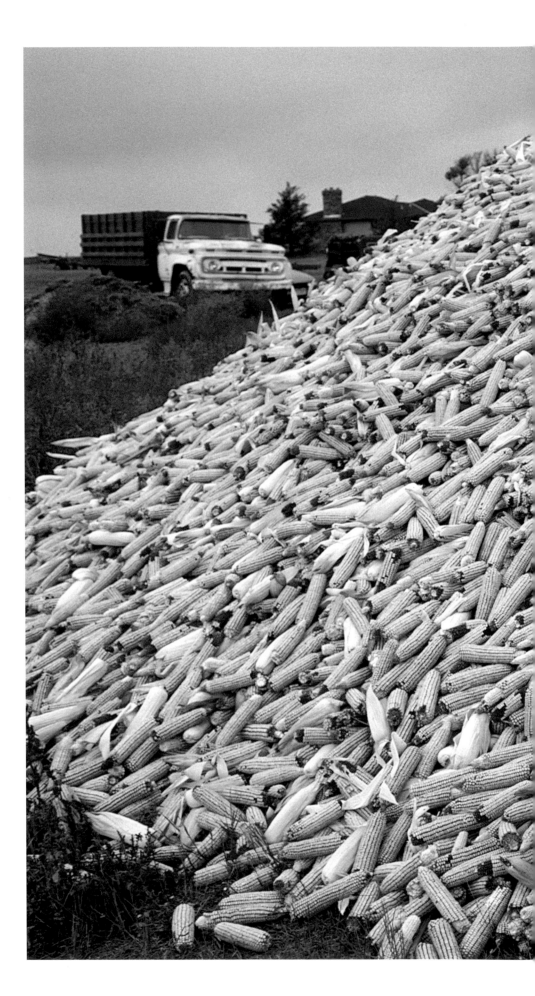

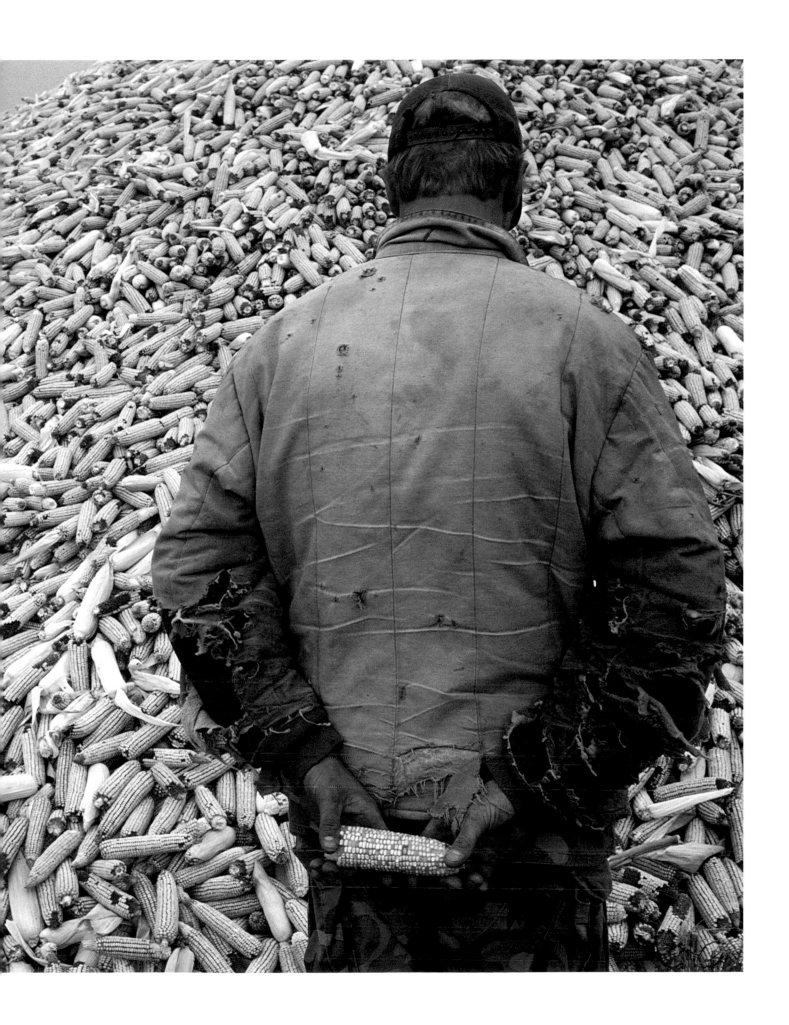

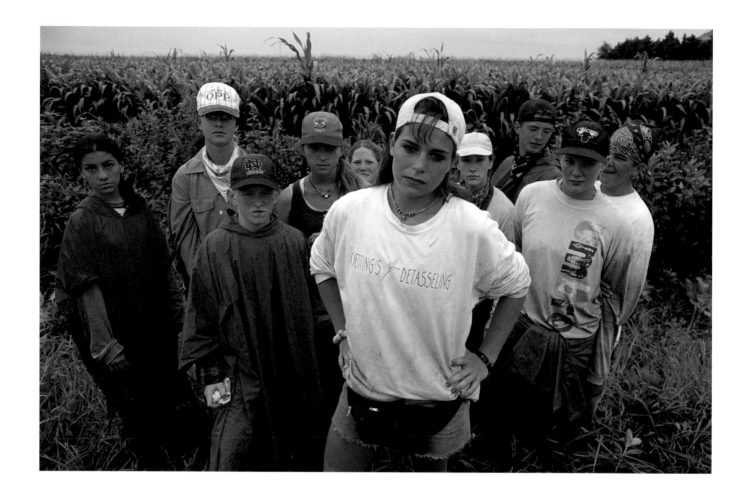

106   Corn detasseling is a big deal to this state. We grow hybrid seed corn here, and it's big business. You have to take the tassels off certain rows of corn in every field or the corn won't pollinate correctly. And it's an odd deal because it's very labor intensive. To do this they hire kids ages 12 and up. Some of these kids were too short and got canned the first day. They missed too many tassels. ▶ The day I went out it had rained a bunch and everybody was a mess. So these two girls, even though they're soaking wet and covered in mud, are trying to feed each other potato chips very delicately. These kids will work in any conditions at all, and if they start to gripe, well, they remind each other that they can make more than $1,000 in just a few weeks. It beats mowing lawns.

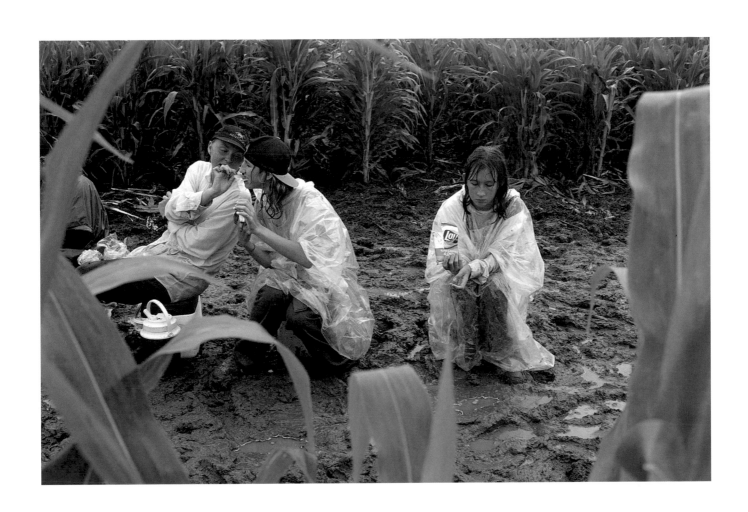

I wanted to get a picture of these kids asleep on the bus because they had worked so hard. But they were wired going home. Their boss, on the left, was telling them what they were going to make that day, and she was kind of teasing them along. She didn't tell them outright, so they're literally biting their fingernails waiting to hear how much they're going to get paid. It's one of the only true moments I got on that shoot.

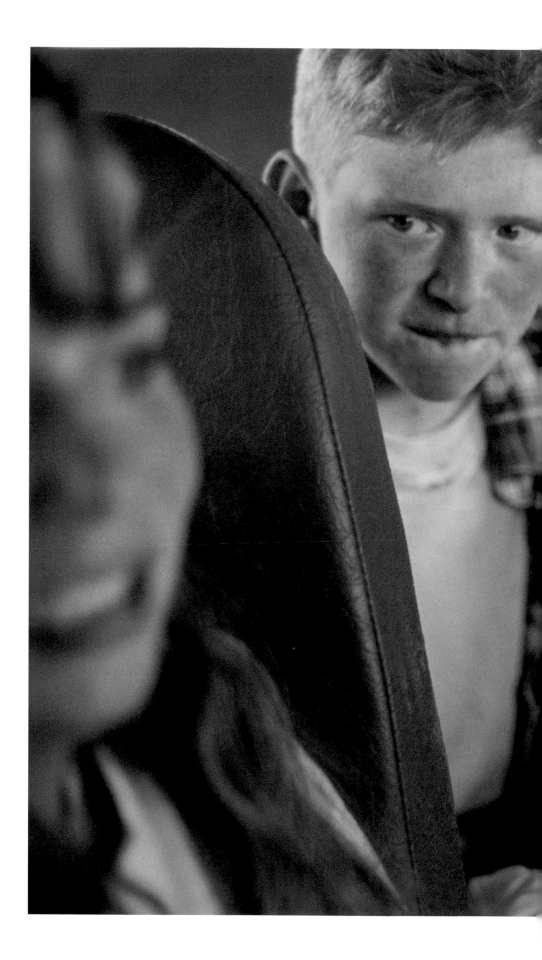

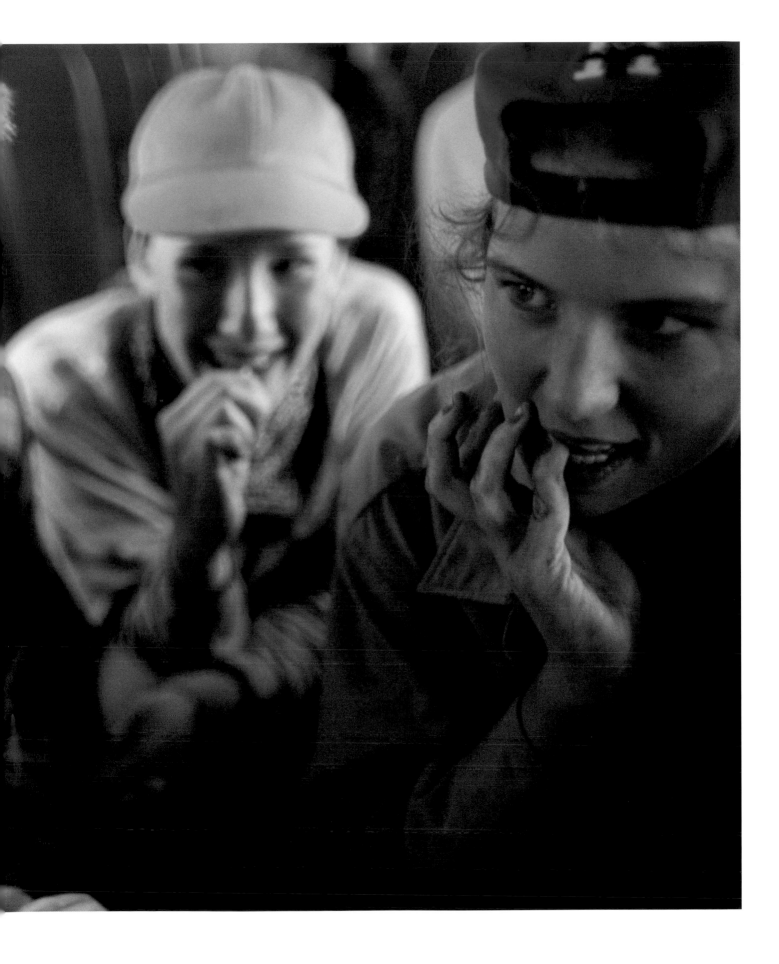

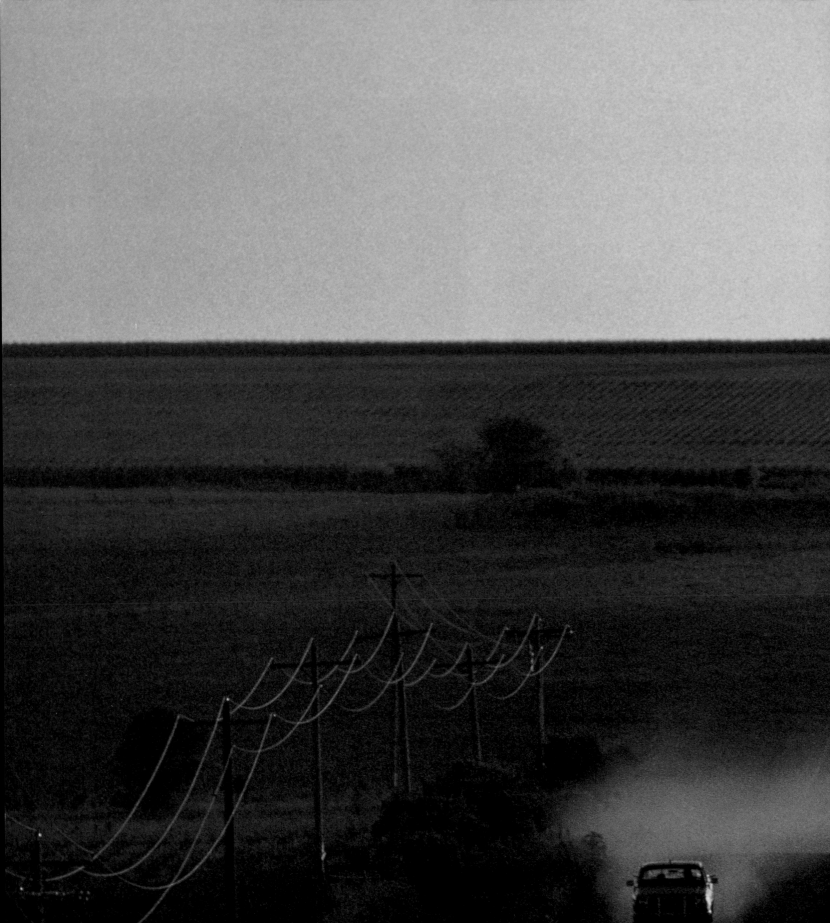

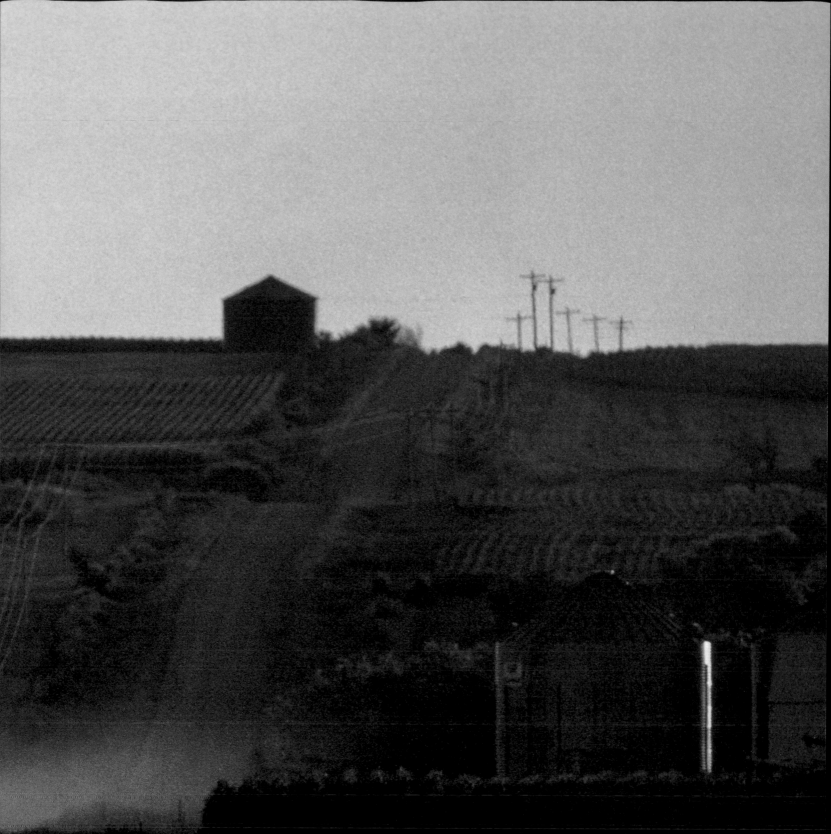

◄ *(pages 110-111)* If there's one thing to remember in farm country, it's to build your house away from dirt roads. Constant plumes of dust in dry times mean that you'll forever be cleaning. One farmer I know built his house too close. Now twice a year he has to put up a ladder and clean gutters that are level full of dirt.

▶ It doesn't always take a rodeo or a thunderstorm to make a good picture. Sometimes, subtlety is all you need, along with nice light and a tender moment. It's too early in the morning to be helping with pigs, much less get your picture taken.

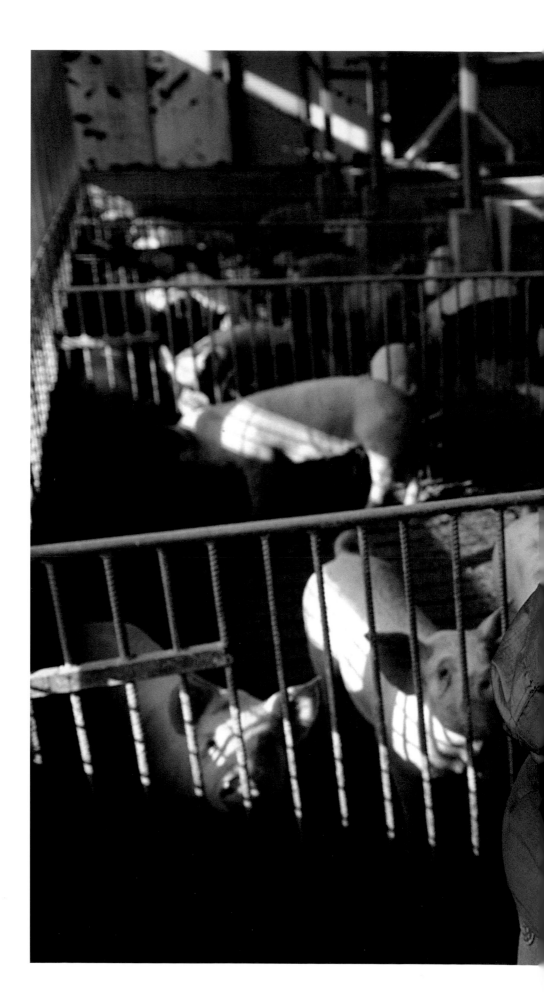

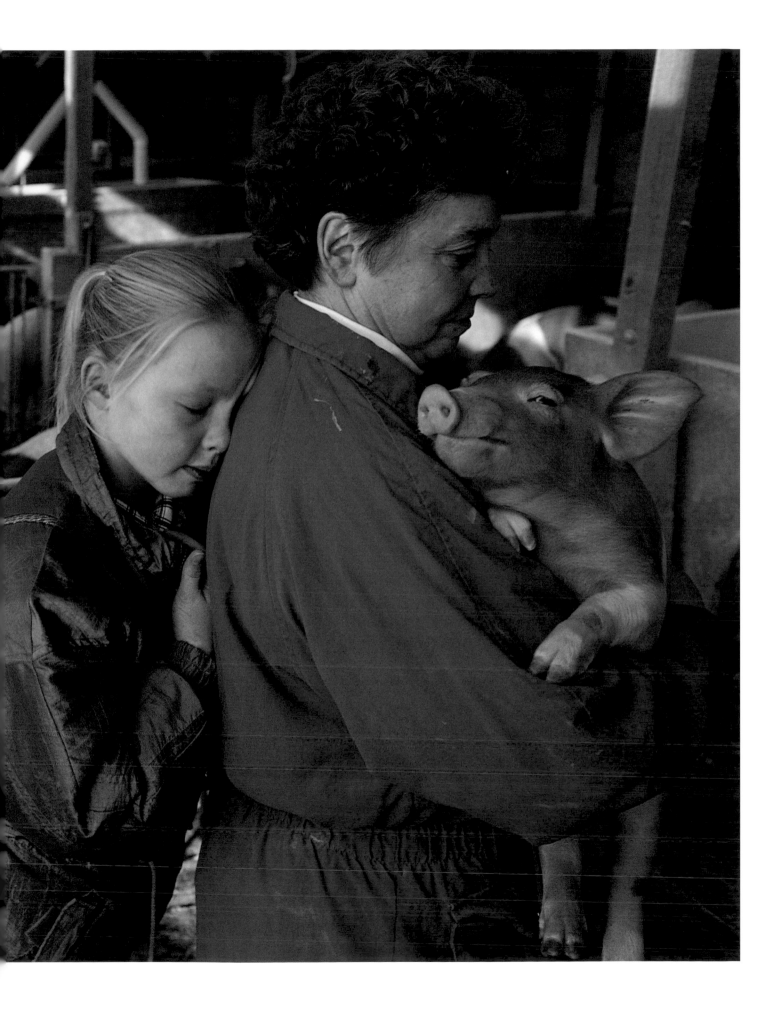

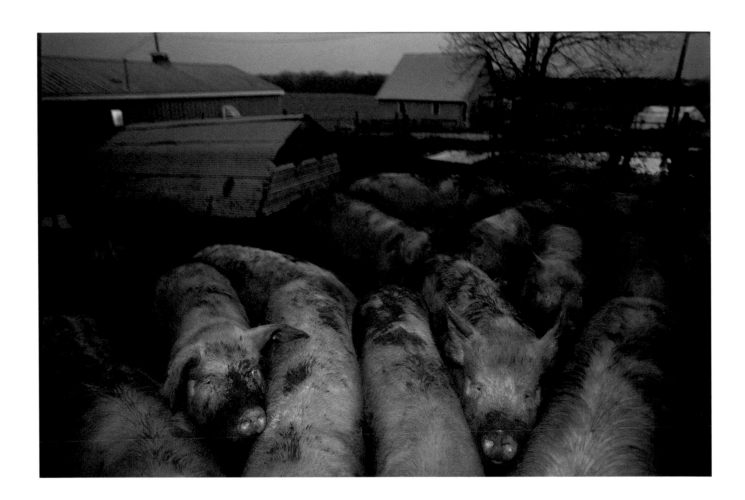

I know I think like a fourth-grader, but pigs are cool. I like taking pictures of them
because 1) they're fascinating; 2) they're always filthy; 3) they're inquisitive and make
impressive noises; 4) they can kill you if you fall into the pen at the wrong time;
5) they make great bacon. I'm being totally honest here. My favorite part about
pigs—the bacon. So this is just a frame taken at a little hog farm outside of Burr.
I think the farmer here thought I was nuts. I was a stranger who stood in a pig pen
half the night lighting his pigs with a flash. ▶ We even have "Kiss a Pig" contests,
and they're quite popular. I like pigs a lot, but not that much.

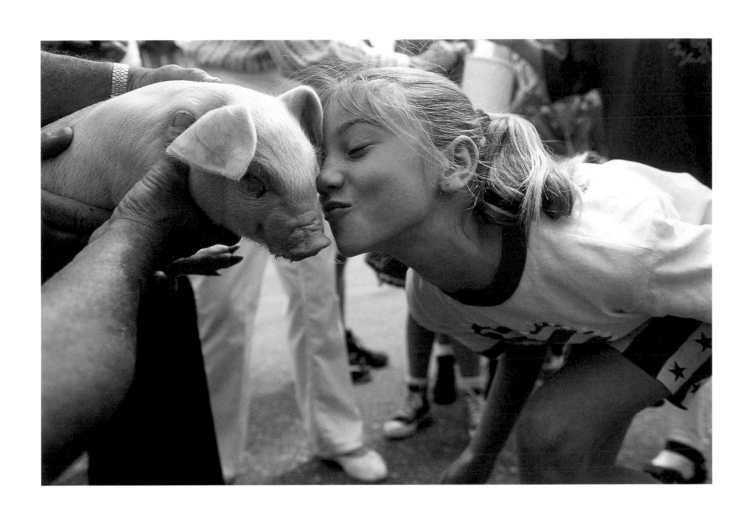

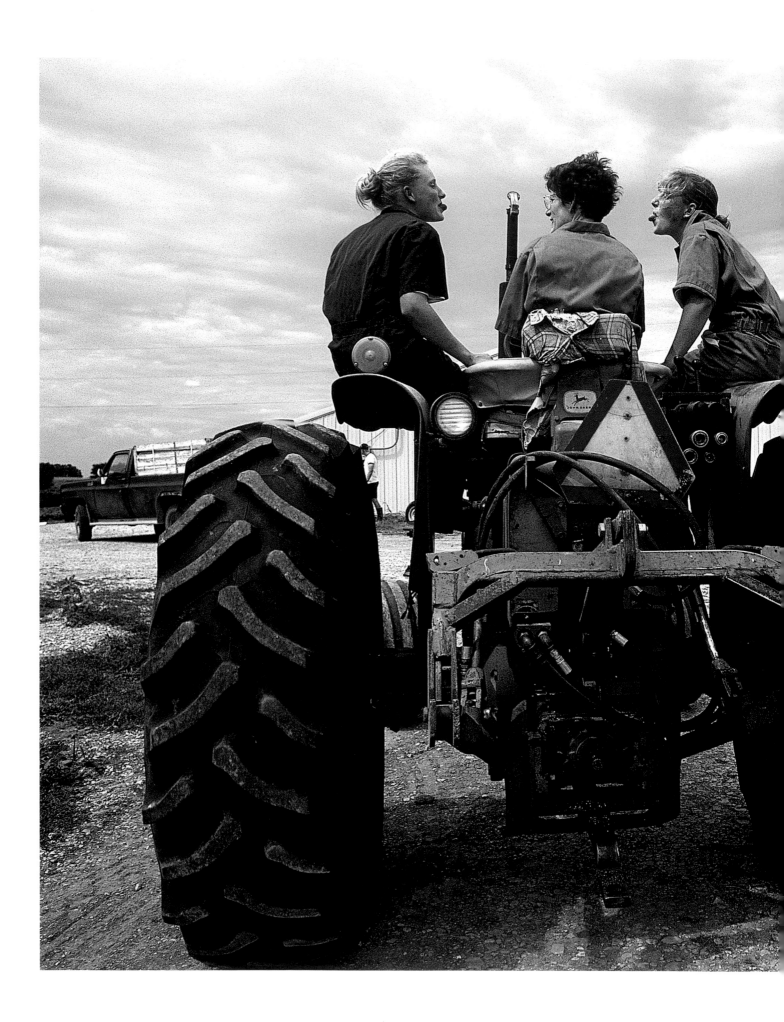

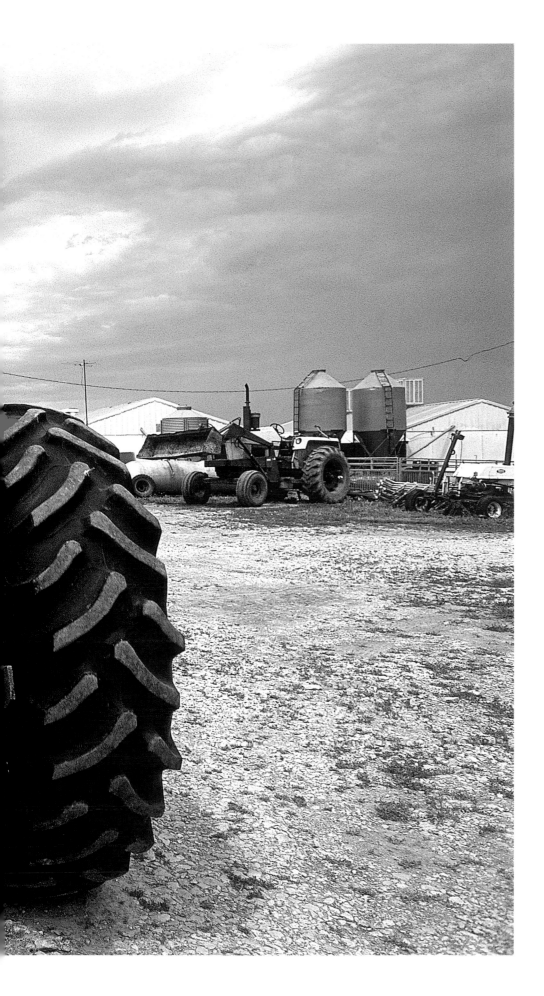

With chores done for the morning, Erin and Mary Montgomery display sibling rivalry at Fine Swine Farm, a family hog operation near Bennet. The Montgomerys use a device that can shoot liquid hog manure more than 50 yards. I'm hoping they use it to fertilize fields.

Someone once said that a

photographer who gets good

pictures out of the Great Plains

can make good pictures any-

where, mainly because there

isn't as much to shoot.

Whoever said that didn't

live in Nebraska.

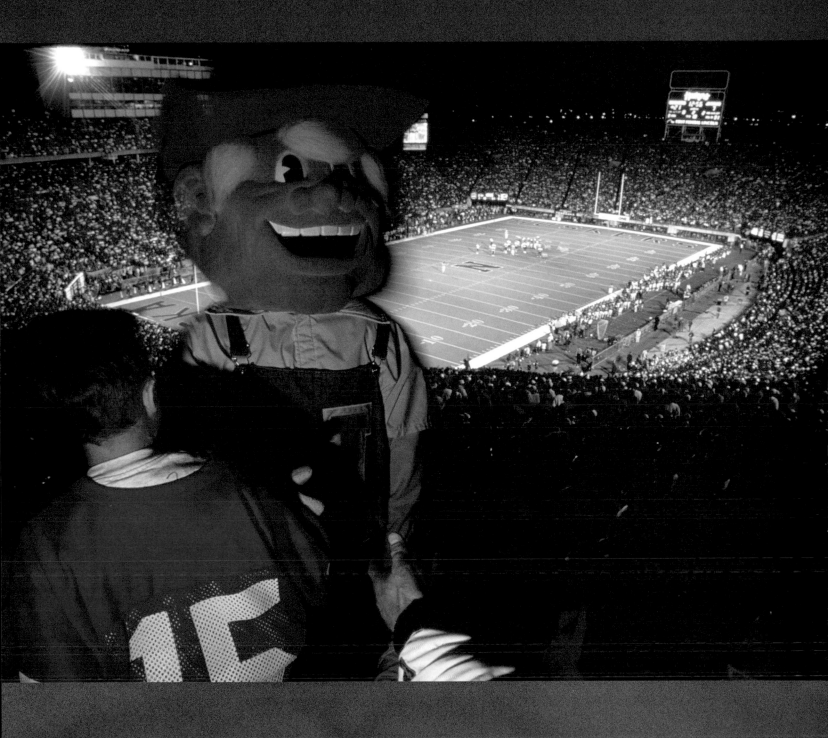

HERBIE HUSKER, MEMORIAL STADIUM, LINCOLN

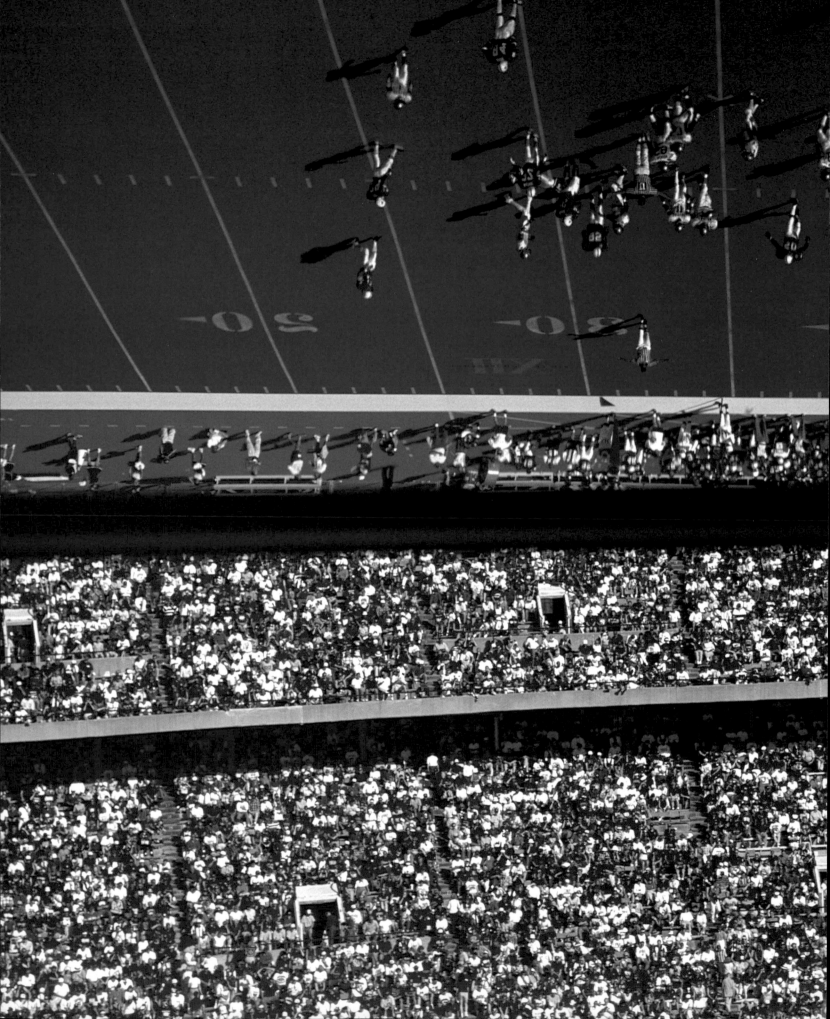

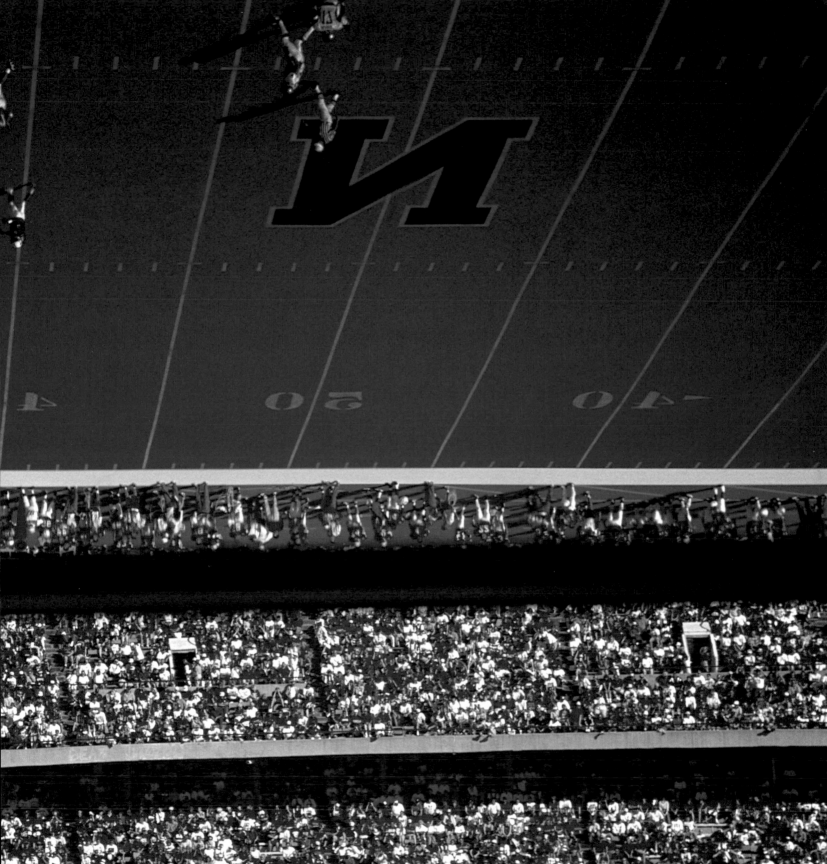

◀ *(pages 120-121)* When you think of Lincoln, you think of two things. You think about football, and you think about football. Memorial Stadium becomes the state's third largest city on home game days when 76,000 people assemble to watch the Cornhuskers. If you're doing a photo essay on Nebraska, you'll get pelted with rocks and garbage if you don't shoot Husker football. It's a key ingredient to our psyche here. My dilemma was how to make a picture that would hold the two or three years it takes to make it into print. You can't photograph any one player or even a coach because they come and go. What you have to do is shoot less literally, perhaps by concentrating on the sea of red-drenched fans with the team reflected upside down in a press box window. My mother doesn't get this picture.

▶ Chimney Rock is a big spike of ancient, eroding rock out in the western end of the state. It's one of the landmarks the pioneers used when they were heading west. Now, of course, it's fenced off and cattle graze around it. It's still standing there, but it erodes away a little more every year. People used to shoot at the top of it with rifles just to see it crumble. Now it has historic landmark status, and most of the time only the cows and a few trail-riding tourists are there to admire it. This horse was fine, by the way. It was just taking a dust bath.

122

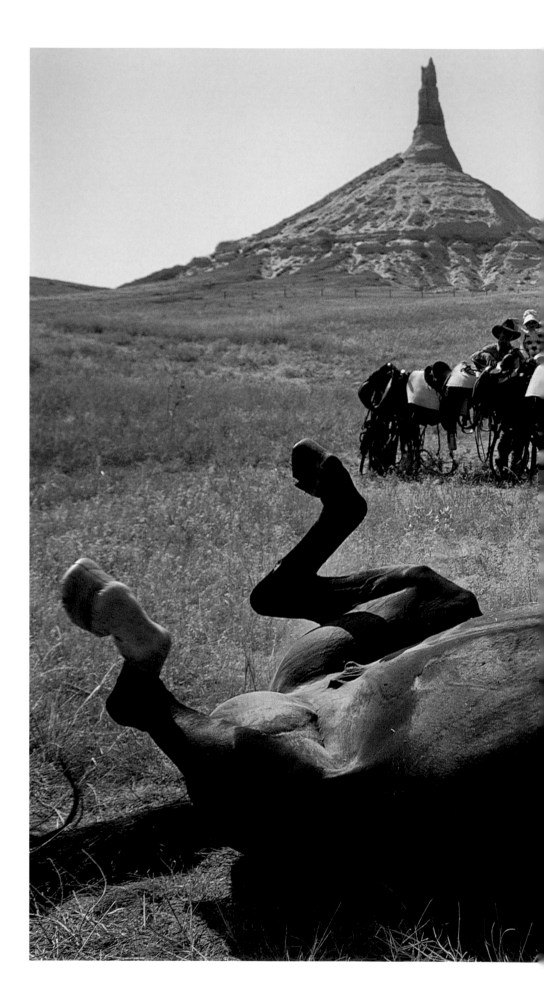

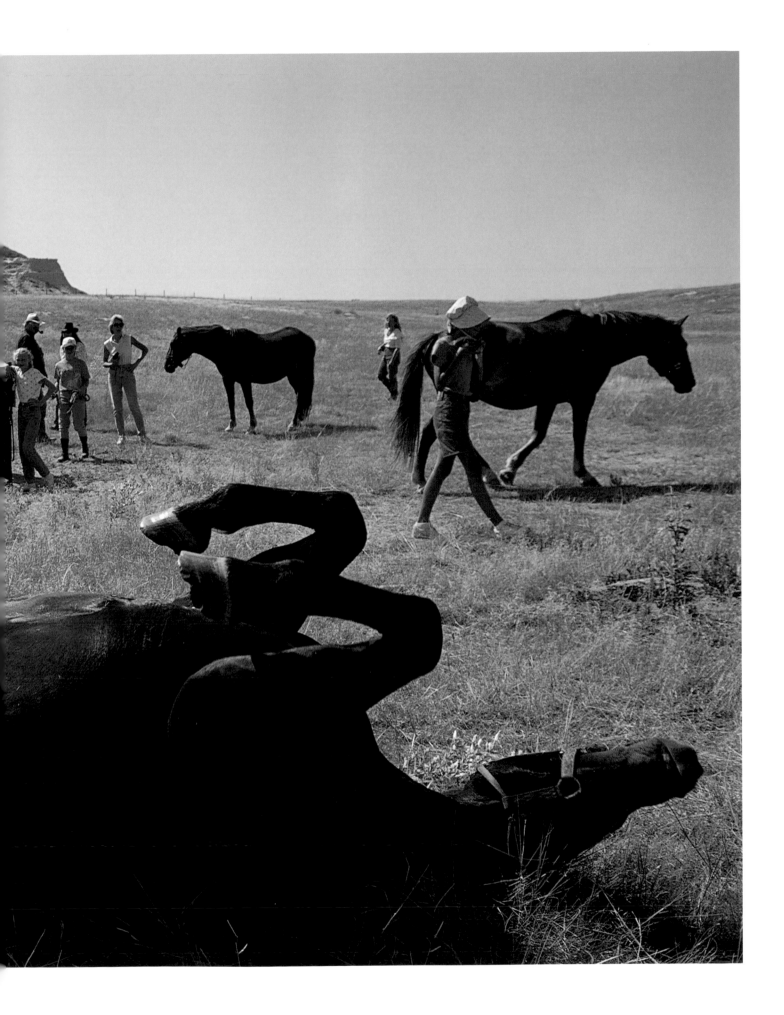

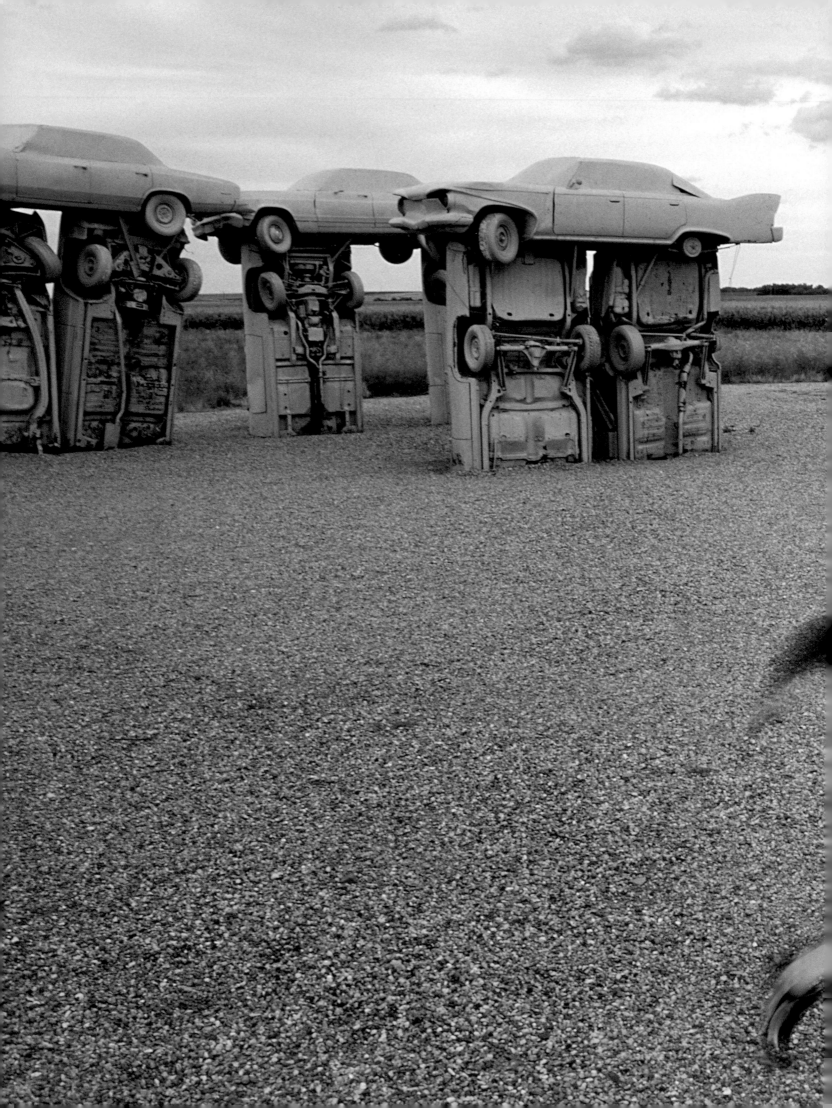

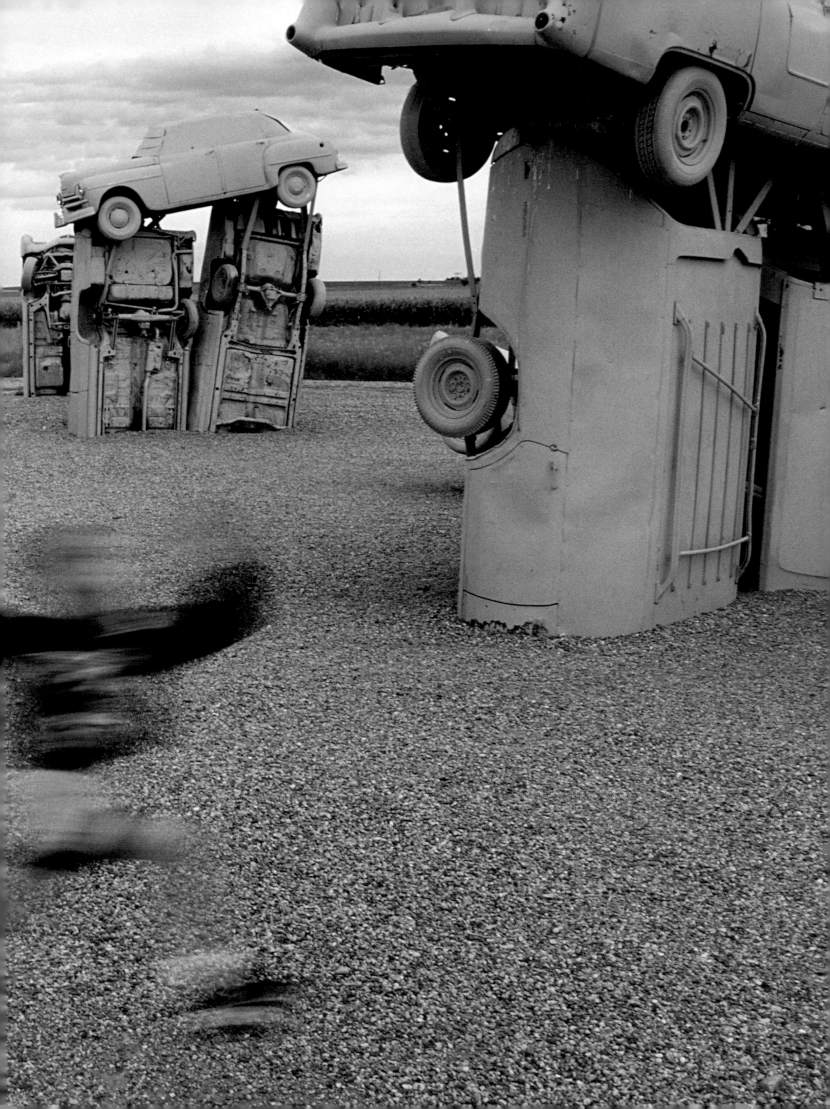

◄ *(pages 124-125)* Carhenge is supposed to be a take-off on Stonehenge. It's a bunch of cars sticking up out of the dirt. I was there three long days. Not many people came. One was a hyperactive boy who blurred past my lens. The few tourists I saw would get out of their cars and say, "We sure drove a long way to see this. Where's the bathroom?" But there was no bathroom. And that was the cruelest part of all.

► Believe it or not, the nation's nuclear arsenal is controlled from an airbase in Bellevue. They have an underground war room there that's shock proof in case something very bad happens. I golfed one day on a course that borders the west side of the base. A big fence with barbed wire separates golfers from rows of military aircraft in the distance. I asked my partner what would happen if I hopped the fence and started running toward the planes. "They'd shoot you dead. Hurry up and putt," he said.

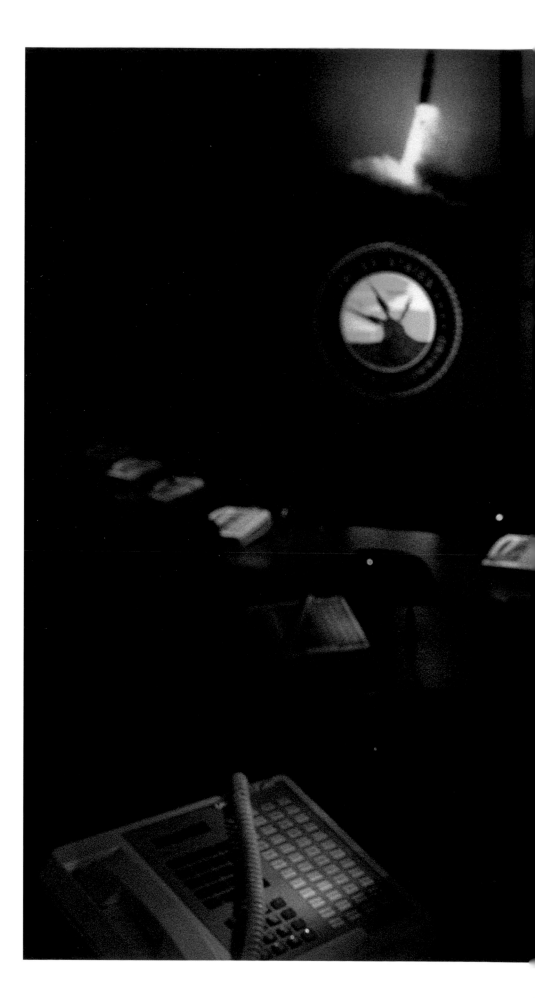

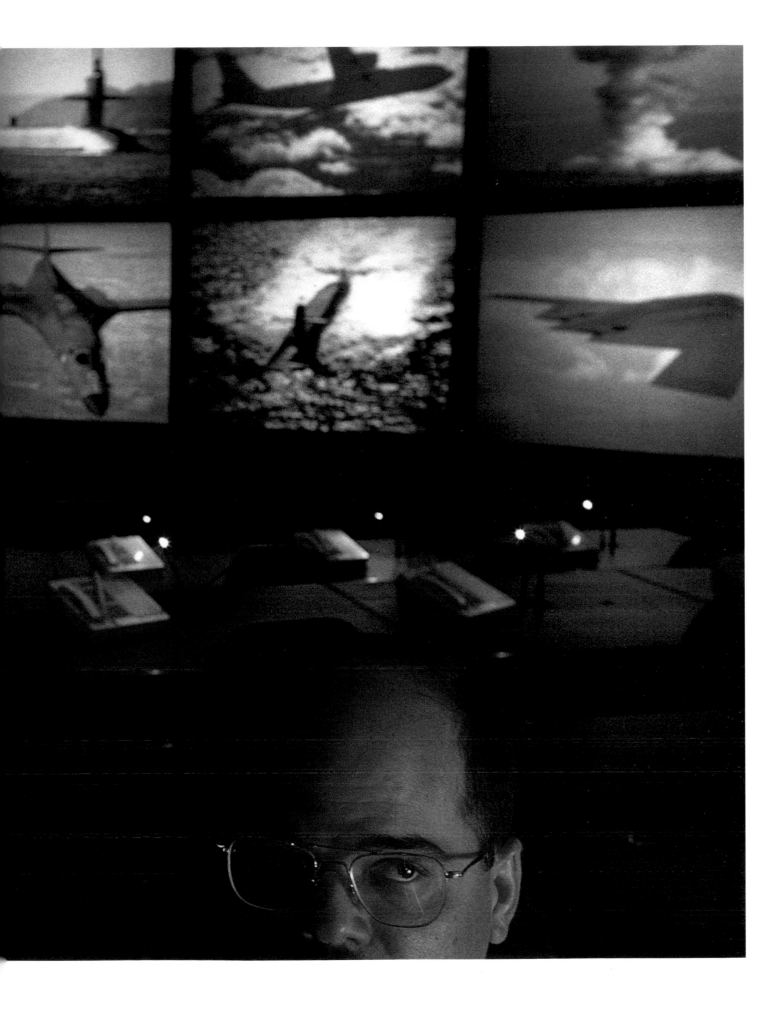

Boys Town takes girls. That surprised me. The thing that I like about Boys Town is that the kids live in family settings. It's not like you'd think in the movies, with wards of the state living in big dorms in rows and rows of beds. Today it's families in beautifully furnished homes. They have a married couple that runs each household with up to 6 boys or girls. The goal is to have as normal a life as possible. When kids first come to Boys Town, they're on a point system; they have to earn points to earn privileges. So their lives are very, very structured for quite awhile. From what I'm told they have a remarkable success rate getting kids involved and realizing that perhaps there's an alternative way of life to some of the awful things they have experienced before arriving.

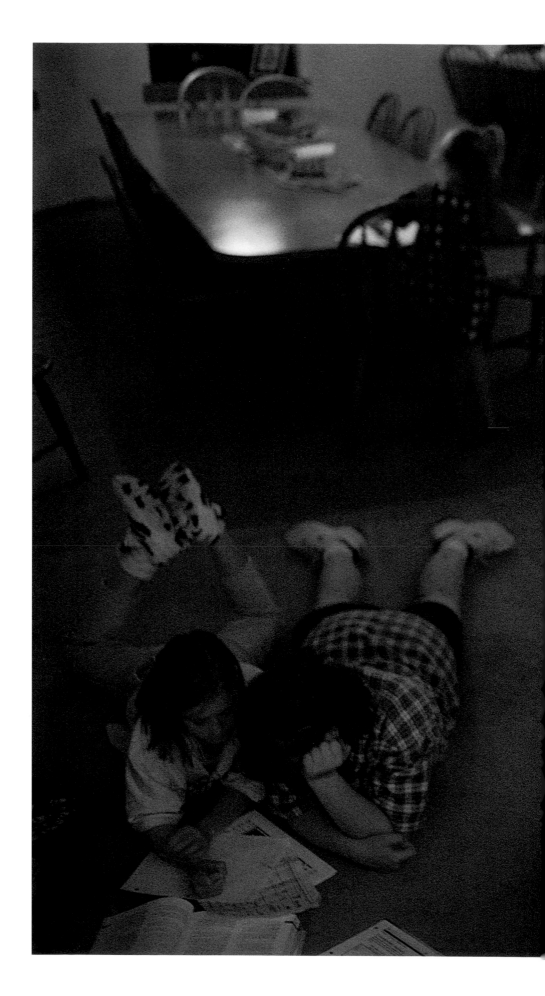

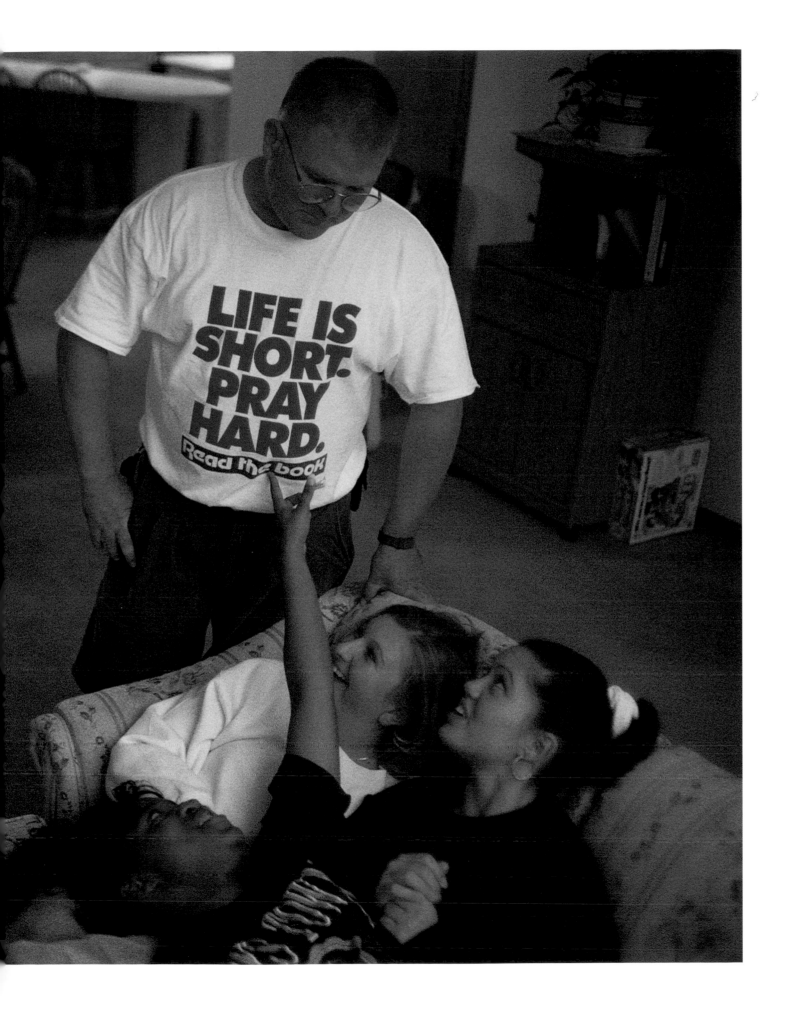

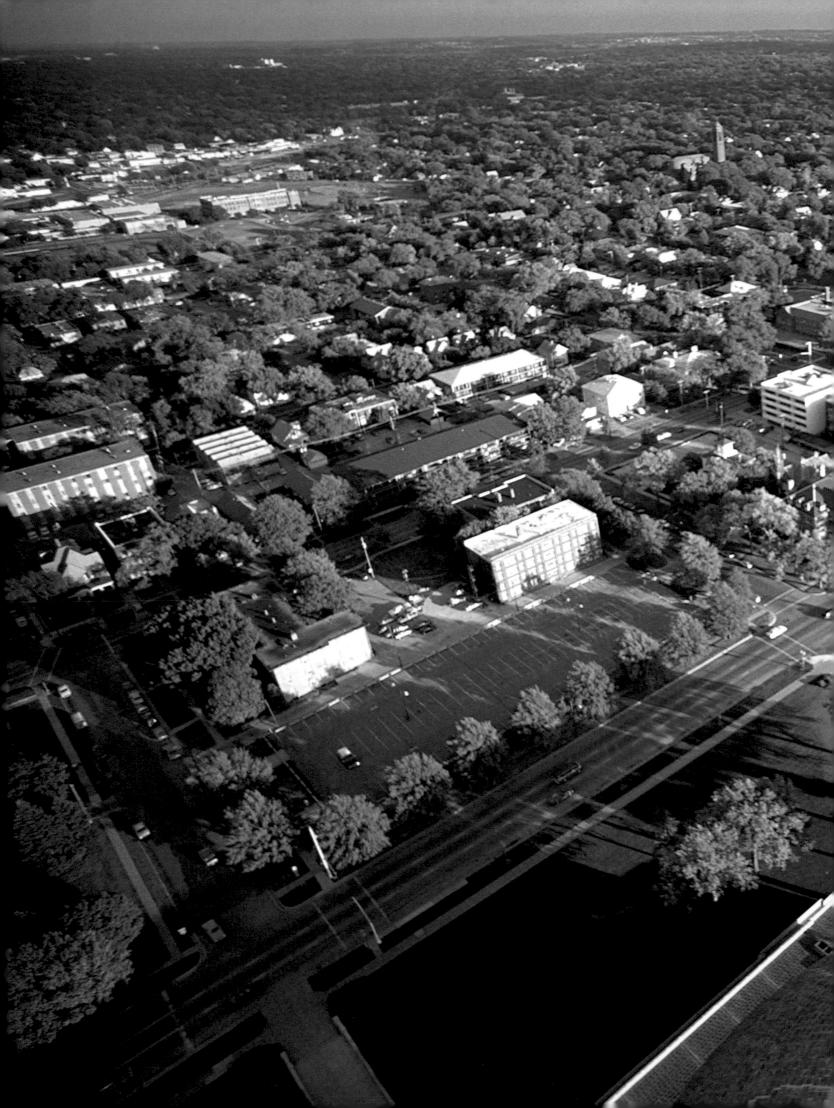

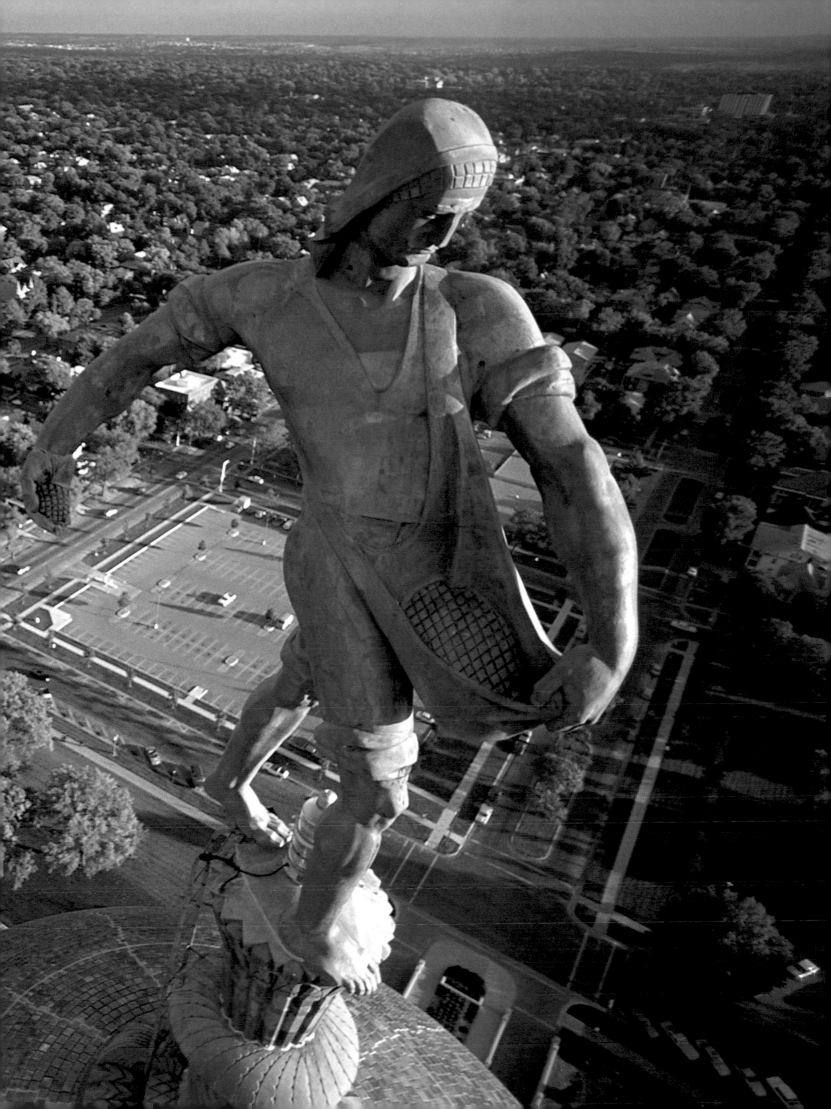

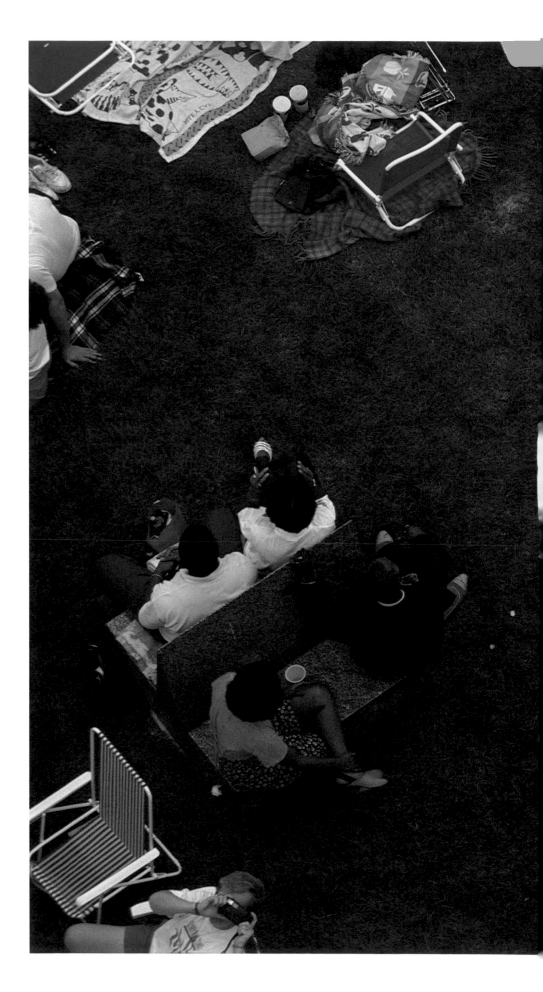

◀ (*pages 130-131*) The Sower on top of the Nebraska State Capitol building in Lincoln is a statue of a pioneer sowing the seeds that settled the West. That day I made the mistake of calling my parents, my wife's parents and anybody else I knew, telling them to gather around the base of the Capitol building for some real entertainment. Helicopters are not a common sight here in Lincoln, so they all showed up. The only helicopter pilot I could find was a guy out of Iowa. I think he flew in Vietnam, and it was a long time between thrills for him. "How close do you want me to get ya?" he asked. "As close as you can." I replied naively. A moment later he had the blades of the helicopter spinning over the Sower's head, the skids nearly banging the statue's inner thigh. "You know," I said, "if we get a little down draft and the blades of your helicopter clip the Sower's head, we're going to die, aren't we?" I wimpered. "Uh huh," the pilot nodded. Good thing I invited everyone I'd ever met to watch from below. Now they had actual proof I was an idiot.

▶ On certain summer evenings, downtown Omaha's Joslyn Art Museum has jazz concerts. I worked the roof of the museum, hoping to go unnoticed. I think this guy had a headache and his girlfriend or wife was trying to comfort him a little bit. I felt sneaky shooting this, but I liked it. See the guy in the lower left corner? He's taking my picture and is about to announce to everyone that there's a photographer up on the roof and that everyone should smile and wave. So much for being sneaky.

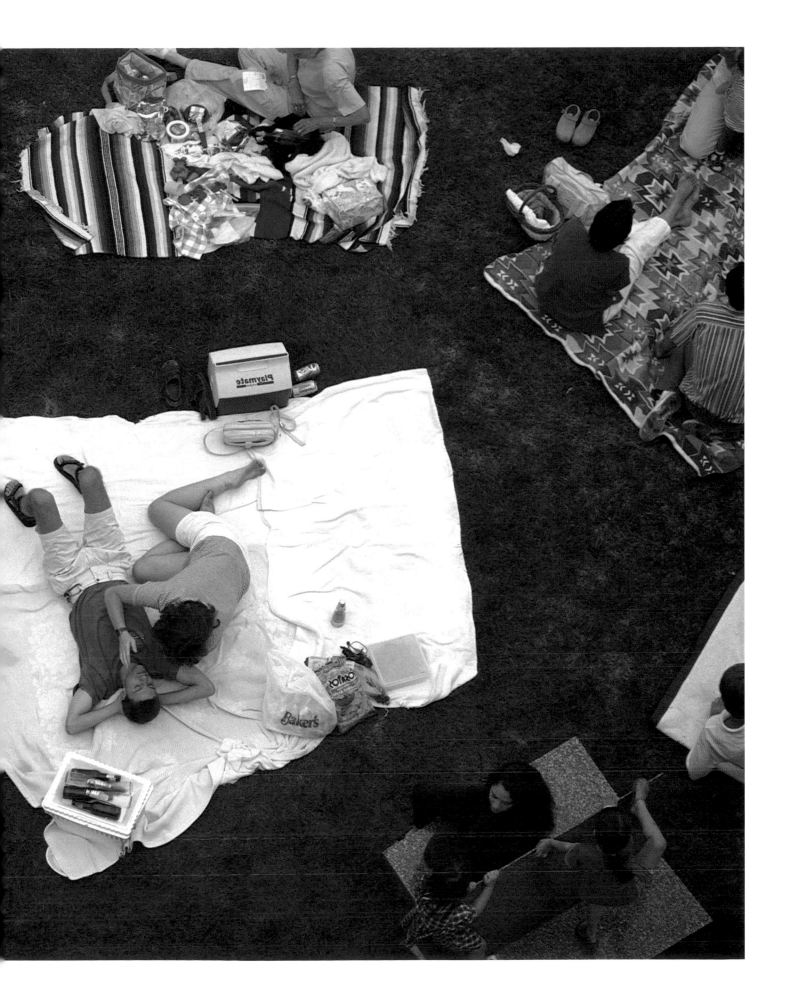

At the Salem Baptist Church in Omaha, the preacher stopped in the middle of his sermon to point at me and my cameras in the balcony. "Uh oh," I thought. Then he exclaimed, "Thank God *National Geographic* cares enough to come to our church." "Amen!" a church member shouted out. Several ladies hugged me after the service. I was welcomed with open arms, literally. I'd never felt so wanted at any church before.

Exposure Note: During the baptism, someone's flash went off right at the moment my shutter was open. In that split second, she did the lighting for me with her Instamatic. That's nothing but luck.

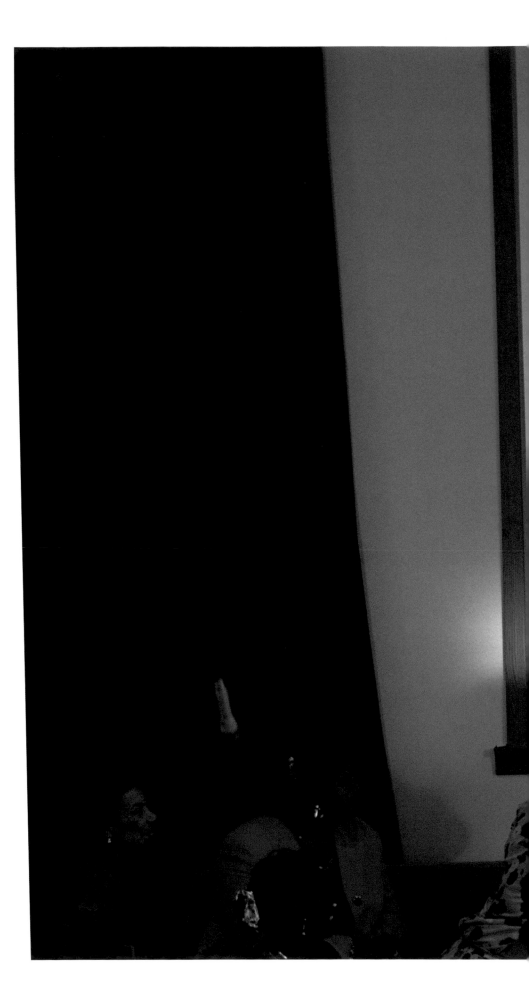

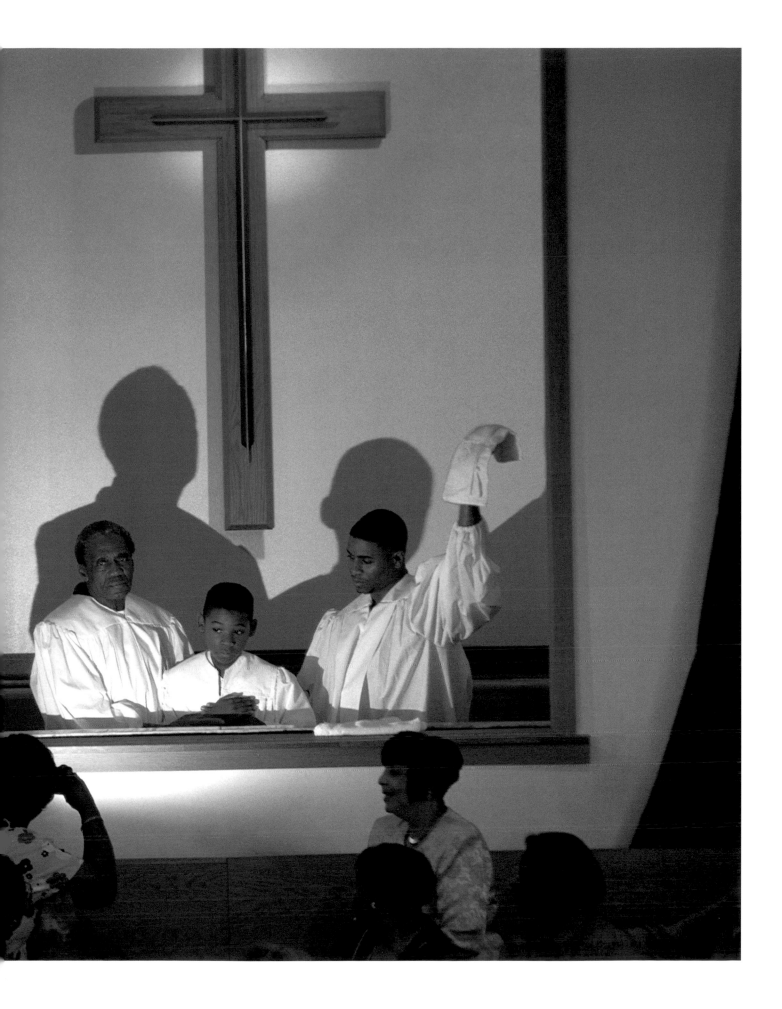

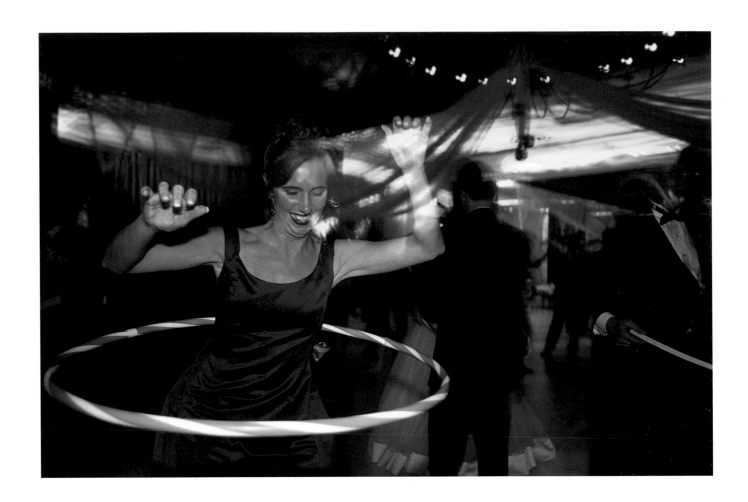

136   I went to the Aksarben coronation and ball for one main reason: Aksarben is Nebraska
spelled backward. It's also one of Omaha's big society events. I'd give it a thumbs up. Hoola
hoops and high society make for good pictures, as do bunches of people, young and old,
becoming royalty for one night. These are some of the wealthiest people in the state, who
devote their time and money to benefit the youth of Nebraska and Western Iowa, and a
nicer group of folks I cannot imagine.

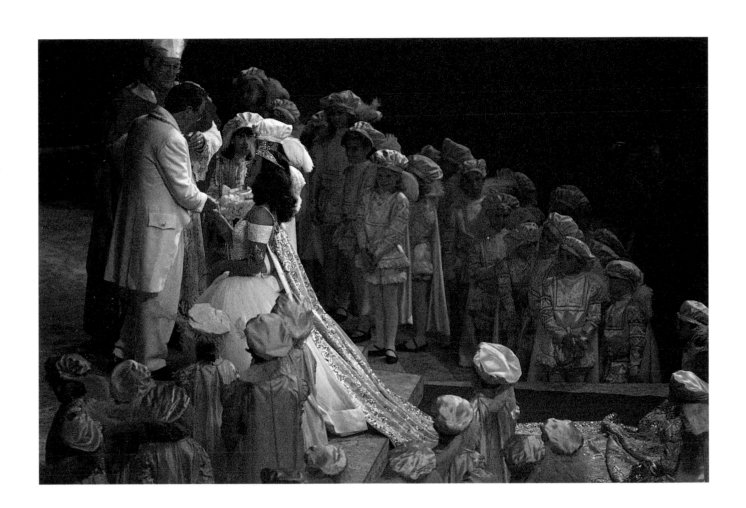

The last light of the day is balanced by
firelight on a Lake McConaughy beach.

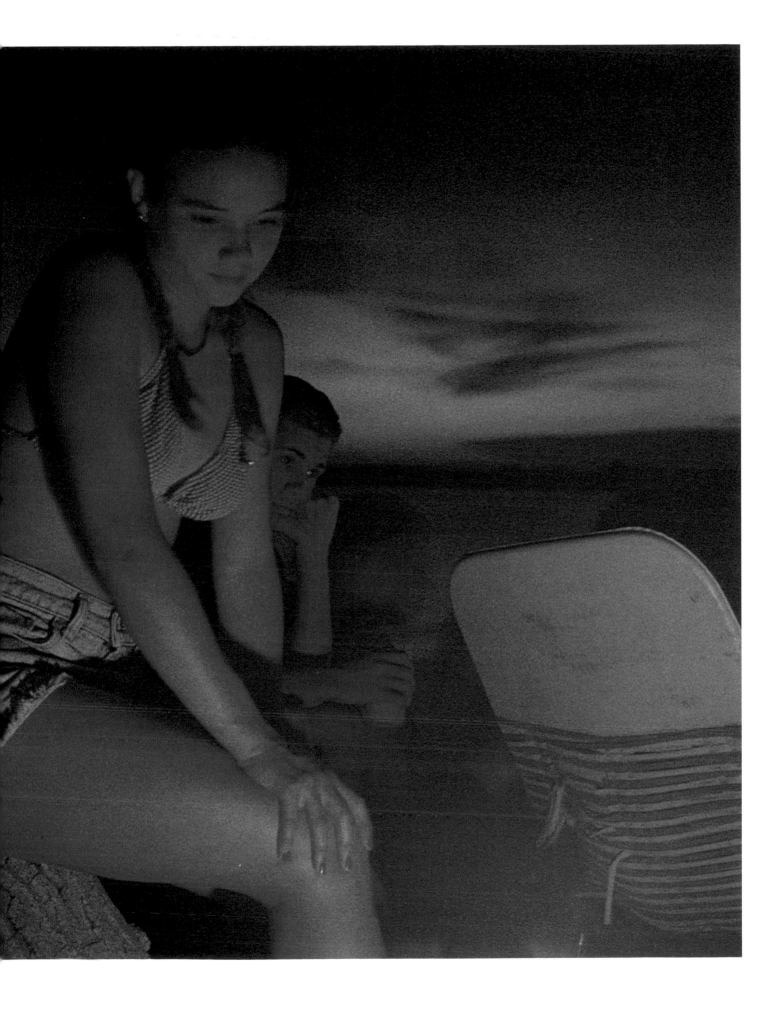

Cliff diving near the Platte River? No… I'm kidding. Here is another thunderstorm, this time near Ogallala at Lake McConaughy, our biggest body of water. People come all the way from Omaha just to do handstands in it.

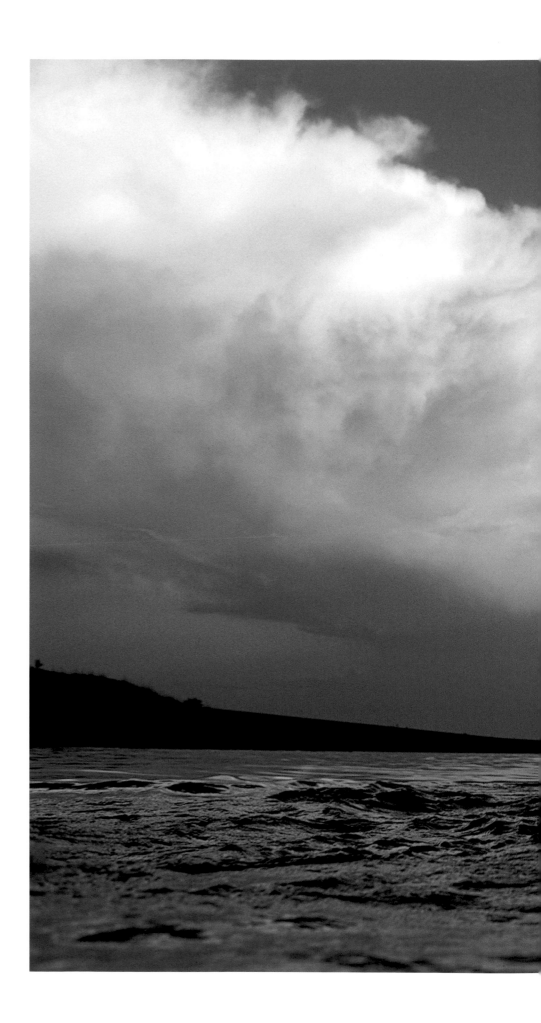

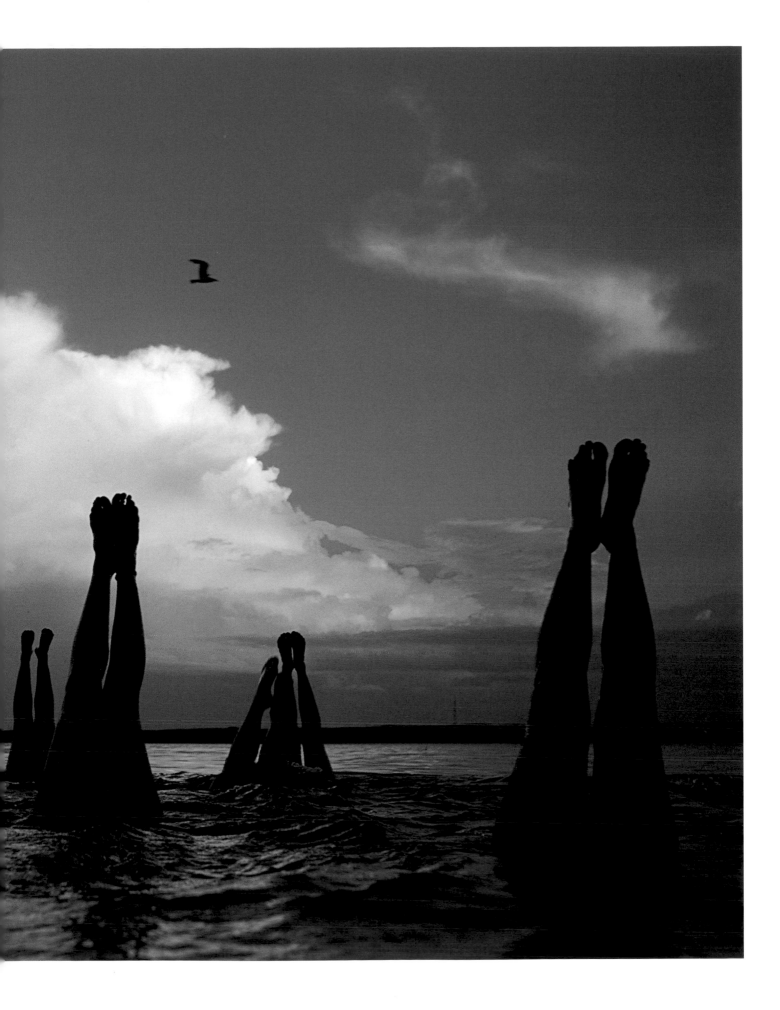

◀ (*pages 142-143*) Much to my family's chagrin, I often take pictures of my wife and kids. This night was no exception. The back side of this thunderstorm was so big that it took up half the sky from 50 miles away. Thunderstorms punctuate our existence here in Nebraska. This time we had our baby daughter with us, who was crying loudly from her car seat behind me. "Are you done photographing us yet?" my wife snapped. "Just a few more!" I called back, hoping to get another roll off. "I don't care if you're done or not, I'm tired of this," Kathy said. "Cole, give me your hand. We're going home. You know, Joel, I really hate your job."

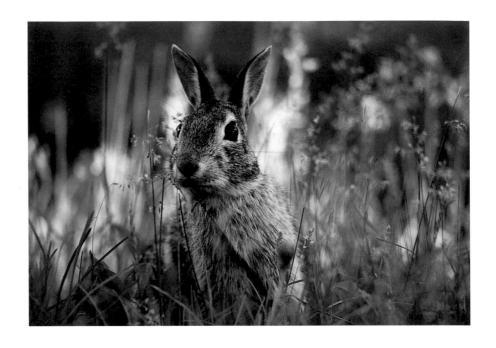

ACKNOWLEDGEMENTS

It's the nature of my job that I'm very dependant on the kindness of strangers. I couldn't have picked a kinder group. Many thanks to all those appearing in this book for letting me peek into your lives for a moment or two.

Also, my thanks to the following folks: Michael Forsberg; Brad Hickerson; Elizabeth Krist; Bill Marr; National Geographic Society; Kathy, Cole and Ellen Sartore; Erik Stenbakken; Tyler Sutton; Tom Swanson; Robert, Colleen and Jeannie Vestecka; Libby Volgyes.

If itching persists, please consult your physician.

—Joel Sartore